EX LIBRIS

C000227504

A SUSSEX GUIDE

WHAT THE
VICTORIANS
DID FOR SUSSEX

ROLAND LEWIS

Embellished with
CONTEMPORARY ILLUSTRATIONS

SNAKE RIVER PRESS

SNAKE RIVER PRESS

Book No 5
Books about Sussex for the enthusiast

Published in 2007 by
SNAKE RIVER PRESS
South Downs Way, Alfriston, Sussex BN26 5XW
www.snakeriverpress.co.uk

ISBN 978-1-906022-04-4

This book was conceived, designed and produced by
SNAKE RIVER PRESS

Copyright © Snake River Press Limited 2007
Text © Roland Lewis

All rights reserved. No part of this book may be reproduced
in any form without written permission from the publisher.

The publishers and authors have done their best to ensure
the accuracy and currency of all information at the date of preparation.
Readers who intend to rely on the information to undertake any activity
should check the current accuracy. The publishers and authors accept
no responsibility for any loss, injury or inconvenience sustained by the
reader as a result of information or advice contained in this book.

ART DIRECTOR & PUBLISHER *Peter Bridgewater*
EDITORIAL DIRECTOR *Viv Croot*
EDITOR *Robert Yarham*
PAGE MAKEUP *Richard Constable & Chris Morris*
CONSULTANT *Lorraine Harrison*

This book is typeset in Perpetua & Gill Sans,
two fonts designed by Eric Gill

Printed and bound in China

DEDICATION

For FZT, without whose support
this volume would not have been possible

CONTENTS

INTRODUCTION

THE VICTORIANS ARE COMING!

L et's imagine a couple of Wealden children of the 1830s clambering to the top of the bell-tower of their village church. For most country children of that time, the terrain they observed would have been their whole world. The village below, and the landscape that surrounded it, would have been all that they would have ever seen or explored. They would be familiar with the configuration of village houses and cottages; they could probably name the families who lived in most of them. The children would see the well where they were sent to draw water and observe the stretch of unkempt open common where their neighbours kept a couple of cows or a few sheep.

They would recognise the pattern of lanes twisting away between the nearest fields, disappearing from view behind unruly stands of trees or hidden by the unfenced woods where they were sent to collect kindling. These were the lanes that in winter would be clogged with mud cut deep with cart-ruts, and which in the summer produced eddies of eye-irritating dust with every footfall. Crossing one of these lanes, just beyond the last cottage, they could see the straighter trajectory and hardened surface of the turnpike road. By following its direction and raising their eyes towards the horizon, they would see the form of the nearest town that they had visited but a few times. The children knew that there was much of Sussex beyond, but the market-day trips and the annual fair they had been taken to once were excitement enough.

From the church tower, the children could also pick out a few small farms in the encircling territory, the ageing buildings worn and weather dented, the fields constricted by hedges or uncleared trees. They could see nothing that their father, or even their grandfather, could not have seen as children themselves; this village world had changed very little in the preceding decades. The villagers' lives were as limited as the territory they knew. Hard physical work was a relentless necessity, but they still lived with privation and little expectation of improvement.

However, the period that followed, launched by reforms in the 1830s, and that we now know simply as the Victorian Age, was a time of significant change that would make its mark on each Sussex village and transform every town in the county. Funded by the success of the Industrial Revolution, motivated by imperial ambition, driven by entrepreneurial inventiveness and enabled by political stability, the Victorians oversaw social, political and administrative reform whilst advancing economically and technologically on all fronts.

Though not always as dramatic as in the industrial towns of the Midlands and North of England, the changes nevertheless permeated most aspects of Sussex life. Thus by the time Queen Victoria died in 1901, the view from the church tower would reveal evidence of the transformation of Britain achieved during her decades on the throne. An Edwardian child standing on the same roof would be keenly aware of the now well-established railway line sweeping in a gentle curve through the landscape, the smoke of the trains first visible as it emerged from a cutting before racing on in full view along an embanked section. The general terrain would be altered in other ways, with many trees cleared, woods reduced and fields enlarged. There would be new buildings in the village, particularly the school she attended and the little Post Office store. Farm buildings would have had additions, a terrace of houses built of brick would now mark the limits of the village and close to the church was a grand rectory with steep, slate-tiled roofs and windows that looked like those in the church. Below, she would also be aware of the hard paved surface of the main street and nearby a neat triangle of fenced green where she played with friends. The old well had

Author's Note

Although this is not intended to be a catalogue of the county's Victoriana, I have tried to be as inclusive as possible for a guidebook of this size. Selectivity has been based as much on pragmatism, as personal preference; accessibility has been an important criterion, so no buildings or sites are included that can't readily be seen or visited. A respect for privacy and legal imperatives has naturally eliminated reference to some interesting buildings, but at no great cost to the overall picture. Where there is an abundance of examples, such as village schools and churches, I have concentrated on selections that best typify the genre, and have sought to illustrate the general with the particular. More broadly, the project of the book is to provide an historical and social context for the entries, allowing the reader to understand the rationale for their original construction as well as for their inclusion.

Visiting every town in the county, and driving hundreds of kilometres between the villages, have been both stimulating and enjoyable; I trust that readers will experience some of the excitement and delight that I have felt on encountering examples of the county's remarkable Victorian heritage – and making their own personal discoveries.

ROLAND LEWIS

gone; in its place there was a cast-iron pump with a long handle inscribed with the name of the northern town where it was made.

The skyline too showed changes. The profile of the local market town had expanded and its centre was marked by the sharp spire of a new parish church. The old turnpike road was much improved, there were no longer tolls to pay and there would be the added excitement of seeing occasional motor vehicles chugging past. There were now the distractions and novelties of additional shops – but on the other hand, there was the disturbing prospect of passing the large, ominous workhouse building at the edge of the town on each visit.

For a Downland child living anywhere near the sea, even more changes would be evident as they looked down over the coastline from the Downs. In one direction they would see a small port with a new jetty and busy wharves where once there was a simple fishing village. In the other, the view would be marked by an expanse of new buildings around the edges of the local town, some spreading inland to the rising ground, others strung along the foreshore road. Here too there were more church spires and towers, both in the centre of the town and in the newly created suburbs. Even more striking was the novelty of the gleaming pier projecting into the sea, its lights at night like an inviting beacon. And out at sea, the horizon would be traversed by ferries steaming back to their homeport down the coast where the railway, glimpsed between the Downs, terminated.

All periods see changes, and it is usually only possible to appreciate their significance in retrospect. The Victorian Age was characterised by a distinctive dynamism, as a period of progress and optimism that is easy to admire. The Victorians were clearly energetically productive and inspiringly creative, so by exploring some of the remaining manifestations of their enterprise in the county we can gain an insight into the values they held and the ideals they promoted.

* Finding the buildings

In the text, names of places where extant Victorian buildings can still be seen are marked with an asterisk *. In the Gazetteer on p.94, National Grid references are given for the individual buildings to make it easier for the visitor to locate them.

INSPIRED BY THE PAST
VICTORIAN CHURCHES & GOTHIC REVIVAL ARCHITECTURE

If you were asked to conjure up an image of a Victorian building, you might well find yourself describing a church with a tall spire and pinnacles, steep pitched roofs, supporting buttresses along the walls, pointed windows with decorative tracery and a door set within a moulded arch – and inside, columns with high arches along the nave, elaborate vaulting forming the roof above and stained glass providing the colour. In effect, what you would be visualising would be a medieval building in the Gothic style that you would be familiar with from many of the great cathedrals and abbeys of Britain, though on a smaller scale. Although there are no purely Gothic cathedrals in Sussex (Chichester contains some examples of the components), there are other village churches built from the 13th to the 15th century with these characteristic forms. What the Victorians tried to do was replicate and re-animate this style, to reproduce the glories of medieval buildings in a grandiose Gothic Revival. It was a project that was to dominate the architectural style of many of the churches and public buildings constructed in Sussex during the period – leaving us with a substantial legacy of their response to this historical source.

Although it can be seen as a reaction against the prevailing classical style of the Georgian and Regency periods, an interest in Romantic aspects of medieval architecture had been developing earlier in the century. However, the strongest impetus for the Victorian Gothic Revival is generally attributed to the propagandist zeal, theoretical writings and architectural work of Augustus Welby Pugin (1812-52). A Catholic convert and an extraordinarily prolific designer and architect, Pugin was determined to revive the Christian spirit, architectural principles and Pointed style of the early Gothic builders, and made it his short life's work. Apart from designing churches himself, Pugin was involved, along with the main architect Sir Charles Barry (1795-1860), on the design of the Houses of Parliament, the theme park of the Neo-Gothic enthusiasts. Influential Anglican 'Ecclesiologists', seeking to reform church layout to suit their liturgical needs by promoting Gothic design and reviving traditional ritual, adopted his philosophy. Thus Gothic became the style-of-choice, if not compulsion, for the Established Church for much of the rest of the century, employed by architects of both great and indifferent skill. Whatever their design variants – Early English, Decorated, Perpendicular or otherwise – the architectural Gothicists found unresisting territory in Sussex and set about their neo-medieval work with Victorian gusto.

Gothic by the seaside

The evidence is most prominent in the expanding coastal resorts – where Gothic spires came to puncture skylines and towers providing new visual points of reference for the townspeople. A typical early example is Christ Church, in Grafton Road, Worthing[*], designed by John Elliott and completed in 1843 with support from the Church Commissioners. This is built largely of local flint (complete with flint chips in the binding mortar) and imported Caen stone, but has many of the distinctive features of the Gothic genre. The windows, which are set in stone, are narrow with pointed arches, in the Early English lancet form. There are pairs of smaller clerestory windows high in the walls of the nave, providing light to the body of the church and Decorated Style windows with stone tracery in the form of intersecting ribs at the east and west ends. All the doors are also set within typically Gothic pointed arches. The roofs of the nave, the chancel behind it and the transepts that cross it, are pitched, sloping down to either side and covered with slate tiles. There is a four-stage tower, strengthened by supporting buttresses at the corners and topped, in the medieval manner, by a protruding cornice resting on stone corbels and surmounted by a protective parapet. The corners of buttresses, as well as the other external angles of the building, are constructed with characteristic Gothic quoins, blocks of smooth stone set in an alternating long and short pattern. The church itself sits comfortably within its churchyard in a small square, giving the impression that it has been part of the town's topography for much longer.

There are other later Victorian churches in the town that are worthy, but less appealing. The large church of St Botolph's in Lansdowne Road, designed by Edmund Scott, originally dates from 1873, and was built in a combination of flint and red brick. A bell-tower, with pairs of tall, louvred openings, and a spire covered with wooden shingles, were added in 1883. St George's in St George's Road, a broad, solid, almost barn-like structure, was built in 1868 by George Truefitt, largely of rough stone, with a red-tiled roof and a little belfry with a spire. The position of such sizable churches away from the old town centre is a telling reflection of the population growth during the period and the importance of the growing suburbs. The church was an essential part of Victorian urban development and church-going an established habit for a significant part of the population. In a resort town like Worthing, adequate and appropriate denominational churches were felt necessary to ensure that visitors would choose to come to the town.

The Gothic Revival star of Eastbourne[*] is St Saviour's in South Street, designed by George Street (*1824-81*) and completed in 1868. This is Gothic dressed in red brick, with smooth, light-coloured ashlar used for windows and other trimmings. The nave itself is strikingly tall, the roofs distinctively patterned with grey and black tiles, and the windows shaped in the late 13th-century style. The special feature, visible from afar, is the attached steeple, a tall tower with a stone spire that exhibits a range of Gothic features. The tower has pairs of stabilising buttresses on three corners, capped with stone where they are angled into the building, and a stair-turret with a conical roof on the fourth. There are blind arcades at the lower level of the tower, rows of arches on the face of the wall introduced as decoration and to break up the plain surface; those above the porch have round-headed arches that intersect to create pointed Gothic arches. At the upper level, there are further arches, this time taller, deeper and with more acute points, intended, as in medieval structures, to emphasise elevation. The stone broach spire itself also follows the Early English model, being octagonal in form and rising directly from the square tower. At the four corners are ornamented pinnacles rising from the masonry, whilst the alternate sides of the spire have sets of small windows, or spire-lights, set in perpendicular openings, and the spire itself terminates in a decorative finial. Everything is intended to carry the spiritual eye heavenwards.

Of Eastbourne's many other Gothic Revival churches, one of the best preserved examples is probably: All Saints, on the corner of Carlisle Road and Grange Road, designed by T.E.C. Streatfield, completed in 1880, and built to serve this newly established section of the expanding town. Constructed using rough-hewn Kentish ragstone, it features a tower with pyramidal pinnacles at the corners of the parapets and a similarly shaped spire. Christ Church on Seaside was built in two stages and completed by 1879. The building is faced with flint that has been 'knapped', split to expose its dark interior, and there is a tower with an attached turret that terminates in a pinnacle – another specific form found in some Early English churches.

Eastbourne also provides evidence that the vogue for Gothic Revival style did not end with Victoria's death. Two churches built during the first decade or so of the 20th century are also in the same genre. St Michael and All Angels in Willingdon Road is broadly in the manner of the early 14th century, complete with a rose window at the chancel end, and the Central Methodist Church on the corner of Pevensey Road and Langney Road has many of the identifying characteristics, particularly the arched tracery windows on the front with 'trefoil' heads formed like three lobed leaves.

Hastings[*] is able to boast of Holy Trinity in Robertson Street as one the county's most renowned and interesting Gothic Revival churches – although its triangular site and town-centre position means that it seems somewhat hemmed in and cannot be fully appreciated from every angle. Nevertheless it is a finely realised example of neo-Gothic architecture, full of medieval character and with an abundance of details to contemplate. Designed by Samuel Saunders Teulon (*1812-73*) and mostly completed by 1859, it was built using rubble stone set in regular courses, and has a wide nave with a steeply pitched roof that forms triangular gables at the ends. The special Gothic features include two doorways with very tall moulded arches, one with a circular rose-pattern window above it, the other with a sign of the Trinity, and a further series of tripartite windows with elaborate tracery, set between the buttresses of the polygonal chancel. There is also a small octagonal vestry, added in 1892, with curving arches over the windows, a parapet with pinnacles and a steep pyramid roof.

The Victorians built numerous other Gothic Revival churches around the expanding territories of Hastings[*] and St Leonard's and about a dozen have survived. But it is perhaps the Roman Catholic church of St Mary Star of the Sea, at the top end of the Old Town's High Street, that is most appealing. Designed by Basil Champneys (*1842-1935*) in the 15th- century style and completed in 1882, it is attractively faced with local flint cobbles. Above the finely formed stone doorway is a large window with upright, Perpendicular-style tracery panels – in the manner of the period being emulated – with a carefully carved niched turret over the gable above. By standing back, you can also see the wavy form of the pantiles covering the roof, the intersecting form of the clerestory windows between the buttresses, and the domed bell-cote. The interior is notable for its rib-vaulted ceiling, constructed with intersecting arches.

The French connection

The most significant Roman Catholic church built in the county during the period is undoubtedly St Philip Neri at Arundel, designed by Joseph Hansom (of Hansom cab fame), completed by 1873, and paid for by the 15th Duke of Norfolk. Situated on the south side of London Road, the building is grandiose in appearance, and now important for its status as a cathedral, but not necessarily charming. The style here is French Gothic of about 1400, and its position on the heights of the town suggests the sort of sight more familiar in France. In fact it is probably seen at its best from a distance, or when floodlit at night. Up close the massiveness is less appealing, though enriched with a multitude of Gothic elements and details. The best of these include: an elaborate gabled porch framed by two piers topped with pointed caps; a row of sculpted figures of Christ and the Apostles in niches; a huge circular rose window; and stepped buttresses topped with decorated pyramidal caps. The interior is certainly impressive, with high piers composed of eight shafts, tall, narrow aisles, illumination from the high-level clerestory windows, and the bright colours of the rose window.

The only notable Gothic Revival church in Chichester[*], St Peter the Great on West Street, opposite the Cathedral, has been redundant for some time, and was being used as a bar when I last had a drink there. Designed by Richard Cromwell Carpenter (*1812-55*) and completed in 1852, it was built, using stone blocks, in the 14th-century style. The windows have the characteristic curvilinear tracery of that period, and a comparison can be made with the three windows dating from about 1320 on the chapel of the Archbishop's Palace across the road, close to the west door of the Cathedral, as well as others on the Cathedral itself.

Carpenter was also responsible for the Gothic style of the original Lancing College buildings (*see p.55*), but, following his early death, it was left to his son Richard Herbert Carpenter (*1841-93*) to design the College's Chapel. He started in 1868 and completed the vaulted Crypt Chapel by 1875, but the work on the upper chapel continued till 1911 – and part is still incomplete. The Chapel has a superb site on the South Downs above the River Adur, and this strikingly dramatic building seems quintessentially Gothic, though with a 13th-century French twist; seen from a distance, or in murky light, it is convincingly medieval in form and spirit. Close to, it is clear that the exterior details have been lovingly and painstakingly created, though this seems more an act of reproduction than invention. The nave is immensely high, with a series of soaring, flying buttresses connected to the building by half-arches and with stabilising pinnacles at the top of each. The elevation is further

Why so many churches?

Population growth during the 19th century was the underlying motive for building more churches; people simply needed sufficient space for worship and churches would regularly be crowded on Sundays since it was reckoned that over a third of the adult population attended services on any given Sabbath. It was therefore in the expanding coastal resort towns like Brighton, Eastbourne and Hastings that many new churches were built. However, with the development of the railway system and the growth of the inland market towns, these places also had need of extra facilities. Both Horsham and Haywards Heath each acquired nine new churches and chapels of different denominations during Victoria's reign and Burgess Hill, six. In the end hundreds of churches were built in Sussex during the Victorian period; one estimate indicates that over 250 were constructed in the three decades between 1860 and 1890 alone.

Other factors came into play, particularly the influence of zealous church leaders or wealthy landowners who provided finance. The 1851 census had also revealed that attendance by members of the Established Church had fallen to less than half the church-going population and the response was to provide additional church accommodation rather than lose churchgoers to other denominations. The new churches were larger and usually Gothic in style, some, such as St Mark's, Horsham, even replacing churches constructed earlier in the century. Both church leaders and politicians were concerned about social unrest, particularly in the industrial areas of the country, and were anxious that the revolutionary movements evident in Europe during the mid-century did not infect Britain. The Church was seen as a stabilising influence with moral authority, so government finance was available to subsidise new building, though not for all denominations. The Roman Catholics still relied on their own funds. In the end many churches were built with comparatively little money or with limited imagination, so many are undistinguished, even if Gothic in flavour.

emphasised by tall, narrow windows and the steeply pitched slate roof. The interior re-affirms the sense of height with lofty pointed arches, clusters of slender pillars and the ribs of the vaulted ceiling. Some of the elements, including a rose window, are 20th-century additions, but in the appropriate style. Even if some think its design flawed or forced, the Chapel remains one of the most exact expressions of the Victorian Gothic Revival in the county. It is open to the public daily 10.00 till 16.00, from 12.00 on Sundays (but closed on Christmas day), and can be approached from Lancing College Drive, a turning off the eastbound A27 by the Sussex Pad Hotel.

The passion for the Gothic Revival became ubiquitous throughout Sussex, much as it did in the rest of the country, and there are some worthwhile examples to examine in the inland towns. The parish church of St John in Crescent Road, Burgess Hill*, is a case in point. All the recognisable Gothic elements are in place, but the variation here is the polychromatic brickwork; basically red brick, but with black and yellow used to create patterned bands on the walls, to emphasise the arch shapes of windows and doors, and make repeating patterns on the walls of the tower. Colour is also used as a decorative scheme for the roofs and steeple, with alternating bands of plain and fishtail tiles. T. Talbot Bury (1811-77) designed the church in 1861, and by this time architects were drawing on Italian Gothic models as a rationale for incorporating colour in the structure of buildings.

At Haywards Heath*, St Wilfred's, in Church Road, stands in terri-tory that would have looked very different when it was completed in 1865. Nevertheless, its elevated position means that it can still be studied and appreciated as a solid example of the Gothic Revival genre. Built of sandstone with red-tiled roofs over the nave and aisles, its special medieval-style feature is the stepped buttress to the tower that contains a stairway, and with an octagonal turret above.

Brighton, Hove & the Wagners

Brighton and Hove* has its own Gothic Revival story to tell, and this revolves around the name Wagner. Father Henry Wagner, Vicar of

Brighton, was responsible for much church building in the town, including commissioning the young Charles Barry to build St Peter's in Victoria Gardens, which became one of the town's landmark buildings. Completed by 1828, it is of course pre-Victorian, but is otherwise a Gothic Revival church. One of Wagner's later laudable commissions was St Paul's in West Street. Despite opposition from disapproving church-men, he purposely located the church in what was then an impoverished neighbourhood renowned for its community of hard-drinking fisher-folk, and he used his own money to develop the project in collaboration with his son Arthur Wagner (*1825-1902*), who was to become the minis-ter there. St Paul's was built by 1848, with a 14th-century Gothic design by Richard Cromwell Carpenter that pleased the critics of the Ecclesiologist movement. Given that the area is much changed, it is diffi-cult to gauge the impact the building would originally have had. Today the dark flint facing, and the patina of dirt on the stonework around the decorated porch, give it a dour appearance against the otherwise bright street scene. However, the tower and spire (added by 1875), which served as a practical landmark and spiritual beacon for the fishermen, still stand out on the local skyline. The distinctive octagonal bell-cote with louvred openings is, unusually, made of timber, but fully fashioned in the Gothic manner. Around it are four sharply pointed pinnacles, and above is a steep spire surrounded by spiky finials.

Even after the death of his father, Arthur Wagner continued the build-ing programme, though not all the churches associated with their name survive. The emphasis seems to have been on size, rather than loveli-ness, and Gothic Revival principles were subdued or variably interpreted. The most prominent is St Bartholomew in Ann Street, designed by a local architect Edmund Scott and completed in 1874. It is an arresting, almost disturbingly large edifice (local lore claims it to be the size of Noah's Ark), built predominantly of brick with bands of Portland stone, featuring a giant rose window, an exceptionally high nave and internal buttresses that form high, wide side-chapels. Its competitor for size is St Martin in Lewes Road, built at the same time and designed by Somers Clarke (*1841-1926*), another local architect, and financed by the Wagner family. This too is strongly shaped and brick built, with a long nave, a few large lancet windows to the front and a row of tall clerestory windows. Not pretty, just practical, in a pack-them-in sort of way.

Numerous other Gothic Revival churches were built in practically every district of Brighton and Hove during the Victorian period; if you spot a spire or thrusting tower from a distance, you will likely find a Goth underneath. Amongst the best preserved, and in no particular order of merit are: St John the Baptist, prominently positioned in Palmeira Square and typical of the genre – with a tower, stone spire and knapped flint facings; All Saints on the corner of The Drive and Eaton Road, a very substantial parish church in the 13th-century style with sculpted figures, lots of fine decorative stonework but a truncated, incomplete tower; St Barnabas, at the corner of Sackville Road and Byron Street, dating from 1883, also designed by John Pearson in the Early English style and built using red brick, flint and Bath stone; St Michael and All Angels, at the intersection of Victoria Road and Powis Road, is actually two churches by different architects, but with a unifying exterior composed of red brick with stone used for banding and thick plate tracery on the windows.

Village churches

The enthusiasm of the Victorians for medieval architecture was also manifest in their desire to restore and renovate many of the existing Gothic churches in the county, a process that encouraged architects to study the original structures and styles in detail. They used old patterns to give Sussex churches new dresses, but didn't always get the fit right. But where a village lacked a medieval church to be saved, a new Gothic one could be created – and quite a few Sussex villages acquired one.

Although it would be unfair and inaccurate to characterise the Victorian Gothic Revival as being obsessed with replication, of simply reproducing the fabric of a bygone age, there is nevertheless some conviction in the conceit of copying medieval forms that is manifest on first glimpsing a Gothic Revival church in an isolated country location. The unwary mind can momentarily be deceived into accepting a temporal slippage of five centuries; without the context of a surrounding townscape to anchor the imagination, the reanimation of medievalism in stone prompts the question: when was this built?

St John the Baptist at Tidebrook* presents one such perplexing image. Designed by T.H. Rushforth in 1856, it is in a delightfully rural position, tucked away in a wooded vale with a brook running nearby and a fine pair of yews to one side. This simple structure, built mostly of antique-looking rough-hewn stone with a steep tiled roof surmounted by a charming bell-cote, has a set of five stained-glass lancet windows facing Tidebrook Lane that runs southeast towards Mayfield.

St Philip, at Burwash Common*, is set back from the road in Oakdown Court. It sits comfortably within the surrounding trees and is another convincing version of the Gothic genre – and a modest structure for the architects of Lancing College Chapel. Built in 1867 using stone blocks laid in courses of varying sizes, it has a wide roof that slopes down to cover both the nave and aisles, a stone bell-cote on the ridge, and a sequence of stepped buttresses around the chancel. Above each of the chancel windows, as well as the porch door, is a projecting hood-mould – a device echoing the shape of the arch and widely used in Gothic architecture to divert rainwater.

The most celebrated Victorian village church in the county, architecturally speaking, is St Mary Magdalene in Church Road, West Lavington*, designed in 1850 by William Butterfield (*1840-1900*), one of the leading architects of the Gothic Revival movement. The building is tucked away behind high hedges and mature trees, with banks of both heather and rhododendrons in the churchyard to add to the pastoral atmosphere. It is built of sandstone rubble, the blocks intricately jigsawed together with the minimum of mortar, and with a red-tiled roof sweeping down to cover both nave and aisles. Sitting comfortably on the crest of the roof is a pretty bell-turret covered with wooden shingles, in the Sussex manner, and the Gothic detailing of the windows extends to the carved apertures of the wooden-framed porch and the robust ironwork on the plank door. Everything about the building's appearance conspires to suggest that it has been an integral part of the landscape for many more years than it has. Incidentally, the churchyard contains the grave of Richard Cobden (*1804-65*), the great Victorian reformer and free-trade campaigner, who was born and died locally.

There are a number of other examples of rural Gothic Revival churches that are worth a look when you are in their area. St Augustine, Flimwell*, is away from the village on the main A268 Hawkhurst Road, in a splendid elevated position, with the ground sloping away behind the church, giving a fine view beyond the graveyard. Originally built in 1873 by Decimus Burton (*1880-81*) using stone, the chancel and shingle-covered spire were added later. Holy Trinity, High Hurstwood*, in a remote position just off Chillies Lane, is robust looking, with a fine stone bell-cote, but somewhat spoiled by the later addition of a timber-framed tower. All Saints, in Church Lane, Danehill*, is full blown 14th-century style produced by the architects Bodley and Garner towards the end of the 19th century. Holy Trinity, in Hurstpierpoint*, designed by Sir Charles Barry, has a tower and spire as well as a commanding position in the High Street, but looks in need of a clean. St Peter's, Slinfold*, is another convincing version of late 13th-century Gothic, not least because it sits at the centre of the village with a fine stone-roofed lychgate to the street. In fact the building, designed by Benjamin Ferrey (*1810-80*), dates from 1861, and replaced an earlier church of true medieval origin. However, the tower, which blends perfectly with the materials and style of the rest, was constructed in 1970, replacing one with the more usual broach spire – demonstrating just how easily we can be misled by our first impressions when architectural details are so convincingly reproduced.

The Gothic spirit

If Gothic Revival came to dominate the spiritual realm of Victorian architecture, there were those who believed that the aesthetic should also be applied in the secular sphere. John Ruskin (*1819-1900*), the foremost art and architectural critic of the mid-century, argued that Gothic contained both beauty and truth and, like Pugin, saw the style as capable of provoking finer feelings: 'All architecture proposes an effect on the human mind, not merely a service to the human frame'. And in an age of poorly designed machine-made goods, he also fancied that the medieval ethic of craftwork could be revived to the benefit of both the workers and the buildings. Ruskin's ideas from both his books and lectures took root, and his carefully studied appraisal of Venetian Gothic in particular extended the architectural vocabulary of British designers. The neo-Gothic stylebook could now be consulted for any form of secular building – and in Sussex it became well-thumbed. As we will see later, the civic spirit of medievalism took new forms from town halls, libraries and hospitals to railway stations, schools and colleges.

Although the Gothic Revival had made a substantial impact, the later Victorian period was characterised by a multiplicity of stylistic choices – all of which looked to the past for inspiration. Even if much of the impetus of the Victorian age was progressive, it was in the area of architecture that the uncertainties are revealed. As writers of the time make clear, the maelstrom of the industrial revolution and the social flux it engendered disturbed the collective psyche. Despite the opportunities presented by new materials and technologies, genuine progressiveness in architecture was limited; no authentic new style emerged during the period that could typify the age. However, whether we like or admire Gothic Revival buildings or not, they remain as testimony to the Victorians' own yearning for the certainties of an earlier age.

Access to churches

Access to most churches is limited to times when there is a service, and therefore not appropriate for casual visitors. I have therefore concentrated on describing the architecture at the expense of the interiors, which may in any event have been altered later, over-embellished or otherwise stylistically compromised. However, I have mentioned or described interiors when there is a reasonable expectation of the church being open during normal workday hours. Given that the internal structure is essential to the architecture of a building, it is worth viewing interiors if the chance presents itself when you visit the site, and make your own personal discoveries.

TO THE WORKHOUSE!

HOW THE IMPOVERISHED FARED IN VICTORIAN SUSSEX

The endemic poverty that afflicted rural Sussex had long been an accepted part of the human condition for much of the population before the Victorian period. Labourers and subsistence farmers' lives were regularly marked by periods of extreme financial hardship, occasioned by bad harvests, downturns in trade cycles and international events. With agricultural labourers susceptible to bronchitis, rheumatism and other debilitating afflictions engendered by working through drenching rain on gruelling tasks, families remained vulnerable. Even a sturdy worker could be worn out by his mid-40s, if he lived that long.

Hunger, and the illnesses it provoked, was a constant and largely inescapable threat for every poor family. High infant and child mortality rates attest to the impact of disease and pitiable nutrition. The only assistance available to combat the menace was through the charitable acts of the better-off, or the parish's provision of Poor Law relief financed by a local levy. In rural areas, unemployed able-bodied men might be obliged to work for any farmer willing to take them at a rate subsidised by the parish, or alternatively they might receive an allowance based on the size of their family and the current price of bread.

For the most needy, usually orphans, the sick, infirm or elderly, the provision was in the form of a parish poorhouse supervised by landed Justices of the Peace. In Sussex, a government Commission of Enquiry had identified appalling conditions in many of these and told of up to 20 half-starved orphans and other children crowded into a thatched cottage at Shipley. Charitable support, whether organised by church or landowners, bound the recipients to display deference and gratitude, whilst public relief kept down the wages of the employed. One way or another the systems failed to address the root causes of poverty, and parish ratepayers – mostly farmers – resented the cost of their contributions. In the half-century before 1834 the national cost of Poor Law relief more than trebled.

The Sussex Unions

Despite substantial opposition, reform came with the Poor Law Amendment Act of 1834, which established both the terms and character of state relief for the whole of the Victorian period. The organisational structure imposed by the Poor Law Commissioners required parishes to amalgamate their provision in Unions to provide large-scale workhouses. In Sussex some 20 Unions were formed. The system of cash payments – 'outdoor relief' – was to be abolished; to receive assistance paupers were obliged to leave their homes and enter the workhouse. But to further deter applicants, the workhouses were to be made deliberately spartan institutions with harsh regimes requiring the inmates to wear a workhouse uniform and sleep in communal dormitories. Further indignities included splitting families, with men, women and children being segregated, separately housed and not reunited till they 'chose' to leave as a group. The rules restricted social contact and involvement with the outside community. Tough financial limits ensured that the diet was meagre and monotonous. At their cruel worst, Union workhouses were just a cut above the county gaol, at their best they might offer some solace for the infirm and elderly, rudimentary support for the chronic sick and elementary education for orphans. But no one would have self-selected for admission if they had any possible alternative to starvation, and the spectre of the Union workhouse remained a real nightmare for the labouring poor for generations. In 1844 one person in every 11 were paupers at some time during the year, either as workhouse inmates or receiving outside relief. A good proportion would, of necessity, have been permanent or long-term residents: the mentally and physically ill, orphaned and abandoned children, the infirm and elderly. For them, the Union workhouse was home.

In Sussex, as in other rural areas, the introduction of the system was spread over a number of years, and there were wide variations in the provision. Boards of Guardians, usually landowners and farmers from the constituent parishes, had to be elected by the local rate-payers, Union workhouses commissioned and built, and a Workhouse Master, typically a tough ex-serviceman, appointed – with his wife possibly acting as Matron. Building work was financed and approved by the central Poor Law Commissioners who produced model plans for their design. One at Ticehurst was constructed with accommodation blocks in an hexagonal form, with further blocks used to divide the interior space into separate exercise yards so as to enable the segregation of the sexes and the division of the 300 pauper inmates into different categories. As elsewhere in the county, workhouses were built at the periphery of villages, both to save on land costs and, more importantly, to keep the reviled paupers isolated.

Union workhouses naturally gained a fearsome reputation throughout the Victorian period that persisted in folk memory until well after their abolition. However, although the melancholic associations might have been a motive for their wholesale destruction, a number of the original workhouse buildings in the county have survived to serve entirely new, usually residential, purposes. We are therefore still able to appreciate something of their physical appearance and dimensions, and, with a modicum of imagination, conjure an impression of the character and ethos of the institutions as well.

From workhouse to your house

One of the most complete examples is just outside Midhurst* on Dodsley Lane, going north on the A286. Originally the Easebourne parish workhouse, this was considerably enlarged in 1836 by the Poor Law Commissioners when 26 parishes were amalgamated to form the

Midhurst Union serving a total population of over 12,000. Now called Budgenor Lodge, the listed buildings have been restored and totally renovated to provide modern apartments and to offer the 21st- century residents 'an exceptional opportunity to experience stylish country living'. The two- and three-storey dormitory blocks ranged around a substantial courtyard remain intact. The original entrance faces the main road with, nearby, a Governor's room and Committee Rooms where the Guardians met for their official fortnightly meetings. The complex also contained workshops for shoemakers, tailors and weavers, as well as a room where old people were employed in the tedious occupation of picking wool. There was even a bathing room and a couple of cells for refractory inmates, though the mortuary that stood by the roadside has been removed.

The original Union workhouse in Horsham[*] stands in Crawley Road (but not the Ring Road with the same name), near the turning for Millthorpe Road. The workhouse, completed in 1839 to provide accommodation for 250, was also built around an internal courtyard. This too is now appealing residential accommodation (called Ashdown Court) for those with a mortgage or two, and its neat, white-painted presentation clearly belies its original purpose. With so many to be built throughout the land, designing workhouses became an important source of work for both local and metropolitan architects at just the time their profession was being established and recognised, and here the London partnership of Hallett and Newman produced an elegant solution to the problems of housing the impoverished posed by the Commissioners and local Board of Guardians – who doubtless had some pride in the public face, if not the internal facilities of their buildings. However, the original façade would have presented a different demeanour to the Victorian populace heading along what was then a main route out of town. Standing back from the road, the classically symmetrical façade has a main arched entrance set in the two-storey central block, flanked by single-storey pavilions with tall arched windows connecting the matching end blocks. The overall composition and appearance, together with the pattern of window lights, suggests a distinct Georgian-Regency flavour, but a glimpse into the courtyard shows the more prosaic face of the four original wings. The adjacent three-storey redbrick building added in 1900 was originally the workhouse infirmary (now St Leonard's), and has a more evident Victorian flavour. Its relative size also suggests the number of workhouse inmates who had need of medical care.

Another appealing residential enclave that has its origins as a work-house served as the Battle* Union. Called Frederick Thatcher Place, after the original architect, it stands on the A271 North Trade Road just at the boundary of the town. This striking edifice, built largely of sand-stone, has a three-storey arched entrance leading to a courtyard flanked by small, single-storey buildings that were used for admitting inmates, and surrounded on three sides by the original two-storey dormitory blocks. Behind a pleasing octagonal tower facing the archway is a three-storey block, which originally divided two further yards partly enclosed by buildings set at an angle. Modern reconfiguration and additional build-ing at the rear has created a contemporary version of a workhouse yard. However, much of the original design remains intact and the architec-tural details, such as the sets of triple-arch windows on the front buildings, can be readily appreciated. On a sunny day, the warm stone, brimming wisteria and abundant greenery makes imagining the grim lives of the original 440 inmates problematical, but doubtless the current residents relish their comfortable community.

Our contemporary estate agents can also offer you comfortable ex-workhouse homes at Chapelfields in Ardingly Road, Cuckfield*. The substantial, and now fully restored, Cuckfield Union workhouse build-ing dates from 1843, and served the same size of population as Midhurst and Horsham; the Commissioners tried to create Unions of similar size so as to equalise the financial burden on ratepayers within the county. The two architects, which in this case included the regional Assistant Poor Law Commissioner, were unhappy with earlier designs that enclosed the paupers within internal yards, and instead opted for open, but fenced, spaces at the front and rear of the building for exercise and socialising. The internal design replicated this approach, with the separate wards and dormitories built back-to-back. The façade of the main wide-fronted, three-storey block was given a classical look, with three prominent pediments at roof level and two main doors with their own pediments and paired columns. The original, symmetrical design was extended to accommodate more inmates and other doors appear to have been added later. The architectural indulgence is that the building is faced with alternating red and grey bricks, giving an overall dappled effect; clearly the Cuckfield Guardians were prepared to tolerate extra expense for the sake of a pleasing appearance. In 1858 a small chapel was added in the grounds, Gothic in style, naturally, and this too survives as an abode.

Providing for sick paupers

Although they no longer survive, two infirmary buildings were added in 1871 and 1890. These final additions to the complex – like the infirmary at Horsham – reflected the growing recognition that many paupers were in the workhouses because they were sick, and that their needs had to be addressed. By 1844, medical officers had been appointed for each Union, but it was not until the late 1860s that reformist pressure and the threat of epidemics persuaded Guardians to recruit trained nurses and provide proper workhouse infirmaries, with these in turn developing into hospitals serving the wider community.

The Chailey* Union workhouse situated in Honeypot Lane, just on the edge of South Chailey village, was built for 250 inmates in 1873 and remains largely intact – though now converted for residential use and approached from Pouchlands Way. Both the pleasant style, a wide, two-storey range in red brick with decorative bands of yellow, and the layout – it had no enclosed yards – reflect the changed design policy for workhouses by this time. The main buildings, with a central archway and small turret with a spire, incorporated a chapel, with a dining room below. There is also a lodge at the front that would have served for receiving paupers applying for admission. The ensemble is notable for its recognition of medical needs with the provision of the large, separate infirmary block at the rear in Shepherd's Way.

A number of former workhouses, including the main buildings at Cuckfield and Horsham, later served as hospitals or asylums, and this medical link is still alive in the still-functioning Brighton[*] General Hospital. Brighton's original status put it outside the direct control of the Commissioners, but it had already an established workhouse for the town before the Poor Law Act and this continued in operation under the control of the Town Council following the town's incorporation. Then, in 1865, a substantial new workhouse was built at the top of Elm Grove, just below Race Hill. Right from the start this included an infirmary, fever wards and lunatics' wards, with further infirmary pavilions added by 1885.

The surviving buildings constitute a substantial, but rather dreary, relic of the Victorian workhouse system in Sussex. The very long frontage of the four-storey main building facing Elm Grove may have classical pediments, suitably proportioned windows and a clock tower, but its sheer bulk and the streaked grey stucco walls evoke dismal feelings – much as they must formerly have done for Brighton's paupers. The original infirmary blocks to the right of the main building are no more uplifting. Built in yellow brick that has gone grey, they rise to three stories with ungenerous windows and only a few bands of red brick to add colour. With some buildings already abandoned or only partly used, it seems that there may be changes ahead. Whatever the future for the hospital, the site remains impressive for its size and position, with a commanding view over part of the city.

Although outdoor relief was supposed to have ended with the Poor Law Amendment Act, some rural Boards of Guardians found it cheaper to continue paying dole to able-bodied paupers who applied and qualified for assistance. Some Unions also defied central government by retaining the old parish workhouses to save money, usually using them to house the different categories of paupers. Even after the establishment of the Union workhouses, the impoverished still benefited from charitable support, and local benevolence prevented some from needing to seek admission. Local sympathisers also did 'good works' within the workhouses, providing occasional treats or diversions for inmates and generally the conditions improved through the period. Union workhouses remained in operation until finally abolished in 1930.

Life in the Union Workhouse

It was tough because it was meant to be. The philosophy was that of 'least eligibility' – conditions were to be less attractive than life outside, so as to deter applicants for places.

The day started with breakfast prayers at six, meals were held in silence and the diet was monotonous. Gruel, a thin porridge, was a mainstay – probably provoking Oliver Twist-like requests in most workhouses – with adulterated bread, thin soups, potatoes and a little cheese or meat. Inmates' official ration was less than that for prisoners of the time though still more than the subsistence diet of the poorest agricultural worker.

In general about one third of the inmates were children. They might get some rudimentary teaching, but hardly an education. In an effort to break the cycle of deprivation, they were supposed to receive three hours' formal teaching each day, plus industrial training 'to fit them for service, and train them in the habits of usefulness, industry and virtue'. However, it was not until after 1846 that funding was made available to train Poor Law teachers. Workhouse children's education remained segregated in this way until compulsory elementary education was introduced in 1870 and they were gradually integrated into local schools. When old enough, girls were expected to leave for domestic service, boys for a trade apprenticeship. One scheme also had boys sent to work in mills or factories in the north, while orphans might be found local foster homes. All their prospects were limited or bleak.

Able-bodied paupers would be required to break stones for road building, crush bones for fertiliser, grind corn or chop firewood. Older inmates might be set to work picking oakum, pulling apart old hemp ropes to provide the materials for caulking ships. Inmates were expected to cook and clean for staff and fellow paupers as well as run the institution's laundry. Until medical officers were appointed or trained nurses employed, those inmates that could were expected to act as midwives, care for the sick and lay out the dead. With exceptionally high mortality rates, the workhouses required their own mortuaries but had little money for proper burials and, at a time of religious certainty, all inmates feared finishing up with the shame of a pauper's grave.

BRIGHTON OR BUST!

THE RAILWAYS COME TO SUSSEX

O f all the endeavours and enterprises of the Victorian age, it is probably the coming of the railways that had most impact on Sussex. It made its permanent mark on the landscape; it enabled the coastal towns to expand and flourish and allowed inland towns to prosper and develop; it encouraged pockets of industrial activity and boosted agriculture with the distribution of the county's produce. By speeding and considerably easing travel, the railways changed perceptions of scale and distance; Sussex became more closely related to the capital and more intimately bound with the rest of the region. But this was a relatively slow process, and the building of the railways in Sussex spread throughout the whole period of Victoria's reign.

Sparked by the invention of the steam-driven locomotive, encouraged by the experiment of the Stockton & Darlington Railway, the Railway Age got up steam with the building of the successful Liverpool & Manchester Railway in 1830. The trunk lines that followed mostly radiated out from the capital, joining London to Birmingham, Bristol and Southampton. Sussex and its towns missed out on this initial phase, and probably for good reason. Building railways was a very substantial and risky endeavour requiring entrepreneurial vision, a major investment commitment, superior surveying skills, exceptional engineering expertise, and a determined group of managers to push the process along – even before the construction work could begin. Initial finance had to be found to fund the preliminary activities including surveying the potential line, and later huge sums would be required to ensure completion. The financial success of the earliest lines (producing returns of up to 10% and substantial capital gains), encouraged feverish waves of speculation, but investors could be destroyed by proposals that failed to come to fruition or might turn to safer but less rewarding investments such as government securities. The cycles of trade and state of national finances therefore had an impact on the pace of railway development.

Lines were built where opposition was weakest and local support strongest, but nothing advanced without difficulty. Objections from the likes of turnpike trustees, hauliers, coach and canal operators could only be quashed by parliamentary approval, landowners had to be conciliated and fully compensated for their property, the occasional aristocrat placated by rerouting lines away from their parklands – and farmers convinced that the trains would not scare their cows out of producing milk.

This was also the age of political *laissez-faire*, so there was no state action directing the building of railways and the network of lines that eventually emerged was the result of piecemeal development rather than design, with each railroad an individual enterprise – though mergers, amalgamations and take-overs figured in the creation of large railway companies with numerous shareholders. However, each proposed line required its own Act of Parliament to gain approval, and the state therefore controlled aspects of the process by encouraging some collaboration, preventing wasteful duplications and dismissing nonsensical schemes.

Sussex on the line

The idea for a line from London to Brighton had hovered around since 1825, but by the mid-30s, as part of the first national feverish rush of Railway Mania, some six schemes were in contention – including a proposal from Robert Stephenson (*1803-59*), engineer son of the Stockton & Darlington pioneer, and one put forward by another successful second-generation engineer, Sir John Rennie (*1794-1874*). All these offered different routes. When the proposals reached parliament, the debates on the lines were lengthy and contentious – delaying a resolution and adding to the costs. The companies spent as much on the parliamentary process as the cost of building five miles (8 kilometres) of finished railroad. Eventually, the lawmakers commissioned their own surveyor to review the schemes and heads were knocked together. By July 1837, the line had Royal Assent and the contending parties shared in the creation of a single company, the London & Brighton Railway, to carry through the work. They were committed to building 41 miles (66 kilometres) of railroad from an existing London line that reached to Croydon, and they were gambling that there would be enough demand for passengers and freight from Brighton to justify the expenditure, given that the town was still comparatively small, and that Croydon was then the only settlement on the route with over 5,000 inhabitants. The committed investors were now required to stump up their capital and would have to hope that the costings were accurate; in any event, this was a vast undertaking and more funding might be required before completion.

Construction was supervised by the engineer John Urpeth Rastrick, with the workforce swelling as the line proceeded; at its peak over 6,000 men and nearly 1,000 horses were at work on the mammoth undertaking, carving out cuttings, constructing embankments, blasting out five tunnels totalling more than three and a third miles (5.3 kilometre) in length, as well as building 99 bridges and two spectacular viaducts. It opened in 1841, offering a fastest journey time of one and three-quarter hours, about a quarter of the coach timing – although at the same cost for a first-class passenger. Suddenly Sussex contracted, the sea was brought nearer to London and the promoters' vision was accomplished. In the end it cost 60% more to construct than originally planned, though within a few years of completion the value of the company's stock rose by almost as much and was producing very creditable dividends.

Travelling the line at speed today gives little insight into the laborious construction achievement and only glimpses of the engineering feats. Cuttings whiz by unremarked, embankments can only be seen or appreciated on the curves, and trains rush heedlessly through the tunnels that took months of murderous toil to blast out. Better almost to catch sight of the line from the roadside or across the fields.

For instance, the fanciful folly that is the Clayton Tunnel entrance, can be seen from a road bridge on the A273 Brighton Road, next to the hamlet of Clayton[*] and near the roadside Jack & Jill pub. The tunnel portal is designed in a classical style and dressed with stone brought from quarries near Newcastle-upon-Tyne; above this perches a mock castle complete with a pair of castellated turrets and a little tunnel-keepers' house.

In Brighton[*], the end of the line, the 366-metre Preston Viaduct, justly renowned during Victorian times, has since been largely obscured by later buildings, but can be observed at close quarters where it towers over the traffic of Preston Road and Beaconsfield Road. The section over New England Road, built in the form of a triumphal arch, complete with stock classical elements such as supporting pilasters, stone capitals, and crowning entablatures, was a clear expression of the builders' own regard for their splendidly magisterial enterprise.

However, the most visually striking engineering achievement is the Balcombe Viaduct that carries the line high over the Ouse valley, echoing the noble form of a Roman aqueduct. This can best be approached by turning off the London Road into Balcombe[*] village and taking the minor Hayward's Heath Road south till the viaduct is glimpsed on the right and the road dips down into the lovely vale. This is a bucolic spot, and the sight of the red-brick arches of the viaduct rising over the green fields appears an alien sight, like a giant centipede loping across the landscape. A marked path at the roadside gives access to the field from which some of the semicircular arches rise, so you can also appreciate the construction at close quarters. Rising to up to almost 30 metres, each span is of 9 metres, and the total length 450 metres; this indeed is a marvel to behold and contemplate – its integral engineering daring overlaid with architectural elegance, including balustrades and the flourish of Italianate pavilions at either end of the viaduct. Alternatively, you could just try calculating how many bricks – made in fields further back along the line – were required.

Spreading the net

By the time the London & Brighton Railway was showing a profitable return, the value and future potential of the railways were already recognised. The Royal Mail was carried by train, troops had been moved around the country to deal with Chartist disturbances, and the young Queen had taken her first train trip. From 1844 there was a second wave of railway speculation and building, the conflict between the competing companies over the different gauges of their lines was resolved, and by 1852 many more national main lines were completed. Sussex meanwhile was still slow in joining the dots of its principal towns. An earlier link from Brighton to Shoreham was extended westwards to Chichester and eastwards via Lewes and Bexhill to reach St Leonard's by 1846, with an important branch terminating at Eastbourne in 1849. The final extension of this south coast route linked the South Eastern Railway Company's line from Rye through to Hastings by 1852. Later spur lines connected this route to Seaford, Bognor Regis, Littlehampton and Selsey. A link had already been made from the Brighton line to Lewes and another London-connected route from Tunbridge Wells via Battle joined the coastal line to serve Bexhill and Hastings. Further building through the 1850s and 1860s brought the railways to East Grinstead, Horsham, Pulborough, Midhurst, Uckfield, Henfield and Crowborough, as well as to numerous villages en route.

Even in the 1880s small cross-country branches were still being connected to the established lines, and the final links were complete around the turn of the century. By then hundreds of metres of railroad had been built, criss-crossing the county; the Weald had been repeatedly traversed, carved with cuttings and encrusted with embankments; the Downs had tunnels bored through them or were penetrated by deep fissures; all the main rivers had been bridged and their flat valley floors exploited; the marshiest coastal levels had been safely crossed. A vast undertaking had reached its natural climax, laying a mesh of connections binding the county to itself and its region. In time vegetation grew back along the cuttings, greenery swathed the embankments and the lines settled into the landscape, as much a part of it as the ancient roads.

Despite 20th-century closures, the majority of those connections exist today. London-bound journeys from all the coastal towns are still using the earliest routes, so any ride on these lines reveals something of the rail-building achievement, even when travelling at speed. The local trains tracing the original coastal route are slower; the lines themselves appear less striking for much of the time, but give intriguing glimpses of both townscapes and downlands. The remaining part of the original line to Lewes now only runs north from Uckfield, but takes in the Crowborough Tunnel that was bored through over one thousand metres of Wealden clay.

Still steaming ahead

Undoubtedly the most popular and character-full journeys are on the two lines that have been lovingly restored by railway enthusiasts. The famous Bluebell Line[1] certainly offers a full quota of steam-driven nostalgia through the summer months and on winter weekends. The original Lewes & East Grinstead Railway line itself was something of a railway-age curiosity, since apart from the towns it connected, the line passed through sparsely populated areas and only one of its six stations, at Barcombe, was near an existing village. This suited the aristocratic Earl of Sheffield and local landowners who promoted the scheme and whose territory was being used; it also enabled their milk and farm produce to be moved quickly to market and allowed vital coal and timber to be brought in from elsewhere. The line closed in 1958 and parts were dismantled; the section that has been preserved runs from the railway's operating base at Sheffield Park* Station (well signposted just off the A275), via Horsted Keynes to Kingscote, south-west of East Grinstead. Apart from the nostalgia-infused charm of the steam locos and period carriages, the trip gives an insight into the Victorian determination to exploit the potential of railways. The serpentine route affords prospects of the railroad line itself, as well as bridges and a tunnel.

---

1. *Bluebell Railway: telephone 01825 720825 for timetables of their trips, or go to www.bluebell-railway.co.uk for full information.*

The other preserved line originated as the Rother Valley Railway running from Robertsbridge to Tenterden in Kent, and opening in 1900. The 16-kilometre section that remains today is operated as the Kent & East Sussex Railway[2]. It runs from close to the castle at Bodiam (though there are no public parking facilities for the station) through Northiam (where there is free parking), and across the Rother to the Kentish side, with stations at Wittersham Road and Rolvenden and a terminus at Tenterden. Again, this is a steam and vintage carriage trip, passing through very pleasing countryside along the river valley, with stretches of woodland on the route and significant sections of embankments through the marshlands. Always a small-scale rural enterprise, the original line by-passed the villages it nominally served; Wittersham Road and Rolvenden stations are three or four kilometres from the centre of their villages. The line came late, just as the railway building age was running out of steam.

Walk the line

Another, and possibly the best way to appreciate the achievement of the builders, is to get on your bike – or walk the line. There are three significant sections of the original Sussex network where the track has been dismantled and the railroad itself retained as a cycle and walking path. Exercise apart, exploring these routes is particularly worthwhile, since moving at human pace gives time to appreciate the terrain being covered and to imagine the effort required to construct the sections you pass along.

All of the routes are readily accessible, and two of them can be joined at East Grinstead. The Worth Way, part of National Cycle Route 21, starts from the station's upper car park and heads east out of the town along the original 1855 line, across country to Crawley Down, with a further wooded stretch before a small diversion away from the line leads into Crawley and the Three Bridges station. The route from East Grinstead in the other direction traces the 1866 line southeast from the town to Forest Row, then east towards Groombridge. Also designated

2. *Rother Valley Railway: telephone 087 060 060 74 for information or go to www.kesr.org.uk for full information.*

The Worth Way, there is access from the A22 roundabout leading out of the town centre towards Eastbourne, but it can be easier to take the first turning on the right along the main road into Herontye Drive where there is another marked entry point. The route to Forest Row is four kilometres; thereafter it combines with the Sussex Border Path and continues to Groombridge.

The longest, most rewarding and revealing cycle or walk route traces the 59 kilometres of the 1861 railroad north from Shoreham, along the Adur valley to Henfield, then northwest to cross the extant Horsham-Pulborough line before continuing via Rudgwick towards Surrey. The route encompasses numerous significant stretches of embankments and cuttings, as well as two bridges over the River Adur. Because of its length, there are plenty of entry points for exploring short stretches; these include Old Shoreham itself, Bramber, Henfield, Partridge Green, Southwater, Christ's Hospital, Slinfold and Rudgwick. Designated The Downs Link, the track continues across the Surrey border to Cranleigh and beyond. Ordnance Survey maps can be useful for identifying the many entry points along the route, and for the cycling enthusiast the National Cycle Network maps are ideal.

The third route that is worth exploring uses the old railroad known as the Cuckoo Line going north from Polegate, right through the centre of Hailsham, on through Hellingly and Horam to Heathfield, with entry points in each place and some at road crossings in between. Again there are opportunities to appreciate the line itself, as well as such incidentals as bridges or cuttings and at Hellingly there is even a path-side station house – now someone's home – that originally served the huge East Sussex Asylum nearby (*see p. 80*). North of Heathfield the line was dismantled, though sections can be glimpsed as Cycle Route Number 21 continues along lanes and paths towards Mayfield.

Stations and termini

The other significant remnants of the original construction enterprise are the railway stations that survive and continue in use today. There are a number that are worth a look, representing a range of the architectural styles prevalent at the time. The termini of the coastal towns are certainly the grandest, expressing the pride the railway companies felt. The original Brighton* Station building dates from 1841 and was designed by the line's architect David Mocatta (*1806-82*). The stucco façade is classical in style, though the later canopies of the forecourt obscure this. However, behind this, the 1881 train-shed is truly impressive. The wide, wrought-iron arches of the glazed roofs spanning the platforms are supported by rows of cast-iron columns, some of them formed as clusters of conjoined columns, much as in medieval cathedrals. The technology and engineering required to create these sorts of spans had already been exploited in earlier termini sheds at St Pancras in London, York and Manchester, but the Brighton version, with its gentle curving form, is still a remarkable achievement. Though primarily functional, the painted ironwork is enhanced with decorative embellishments, including floriated capitals and rosette motifs on the columns, and openwork designs featuring the Brighton crest on the spandrels bracing the roof. The engineering of the station is also remarkable by virtue of its position; the structure stands 40 metres above sea level, on an artificial plateau that had to be cut laboriously from the chalk ridge. The seaward view from the entrance down Queen's Road provides a graphic illustration of the achievement.

Eastbourne* got its first terminal station in 1849, with the completion of the through route to London. This was later replaced, and the current terminus (at the junction of Upperton Road and Ashford Road), designed by F.D. Bannister, dates from 1886. This is a delightful blend of fanciful and idiosyncratic architecture with the pragmatic – since its design still functions well as a station. Built in distinctive yellow brick, the street-side façade is low, with a set of glazed canopies supported by cast-iron columns complete with decorative capitals and brackets – painted the original bright blue and yellow. Rising above these at the apex of the frontage is a splendid, two-stage clock tower topped with a sharply inclined pyramidal roof. The other striking features are two large roofs, both with a distinctly French feeling. One is hipped, with scalloped grey tiling and gently curved, rising to a platform with decorative railings and a flagpole; the other rises above an upper floor with arched

WHAT THE VICTORIANS DID FOR SUSSEX

The navvies – the men who really built the railways

Navvies were mostly itinerants, moving around the country from line to line as the work was completed. They lived near the routes in shanties, encampments of improvised shelters constructed using mud, stone and timber, or wooden huts with tarpaulin roofs. They may have had women and families with them or shared huts as a group; a few found lodgings in local villages. Otherwise often living in isolated locations, the heavy-eating navvies were readily exploited by the contractors who set up their own truck shops to sell them food at inflated prices. Payday was once a month, usually paid at a pub and this was invariably followed by bouts of drinking. Beer was part of the staple diet and strong liquor was often consumed whilst working, leading to recklessness and more accidents. Navvies had a reputation for ferocious behaviour, brutal language and ready violence, much of it attributed to alcohol, and local communities often feared them.

windows to form a delightful pavilion structure, it too being topped by a platform. The station concourse has also been well preserved. The yellow brick adds to the bright, open feeling created by the overhead glazing, and the arches of the rows of windows and doors are emphasised with red brick. In all, a building redolent of the Victorian success with the building of the railways and well worth encountering.

Of the inland stations, Lewes and Battle are perhaps the most significant. The appearance of Lewes's* surviving 1885 station (in Station Road) has more than a little in common with Eastbourne's. This too is of yellow brick, with a glazed canopy along the façade, and the window and door arches emphasised in red brick with stone mouldings and keystones. There are several interesting period details including the cast-iron columns supporting the canopy, original lamps on wall brackets and stonework with decorative foliage carvings. The façade also has a stone parapet pierced by a continuous row of circular apertures, topped by some curious looking urns. The other big features are a hipped roof rising to a glazed lantern that provides light to the hall below, and a series of bold canopies over the platforms supported by cast-iron columns. For a railway station, this is a building with character and some charm.

By contrast, the stone-built Battle* Station is pure Gothic Revival, complete with Early English-style rib-work tracery in the upper parts of the booking hall windows and a porch with a pointed arch doorway. In fact the first impression is of a chapel, with accommodation provided in the attached two-storey section, though nowadays the ecclesiastical fancy is undercut by the car park full of shiny commuter vehicles. Nevertheless, this is a beautifully composed building, where all the details seem comfortingly apposite; there are alternating bands of straight and rounded tiles on the steeply pitched roofs, which are also topped with decorative ridge tiles. The domestic aspect is manifest by tall chimney stacks, a pretty dormer window, diamond-pattern glazing; even the waiting room has chapel-like windows and an open timber roof. The Revival theme continues with pointed Gothic arches through to the platforms. Designed by W. Trees, the line's architect, it opened in 1852 and can be found just off Battle Hill, the A2100 Hastings Road. Worth seeing for its own sake, although, of course, Battle is always rewarding to visit.

Apart from the Bluebell Line's well-preserved Sheffield Park Station, few Victorian country stations survive sufficiently intact. However, there is an appealing stone-built station house at Etchingham (on the A265) that has a strong residential feel to it as originally railway staff lived in part of it. Opened in 1852, and also designed by Trees, it has several tall chimneys, a red-tiled roof, and porches to the doors; the platform side also has distinctive Tudor-style doorways and a canopy supported by iron trusses.

Working on the railroad

A pick, a shovel, a barrow and a barrel of gunpowder were the tools of the trade of the small army of labourers who moved around the country building the Victorian railroads. Originating with earlier generations of 'navigators' who constructed the canals and some turnpike roads, these were a tough breed undertaking the toughest of tasks. They included Irish immigrants, Scots and men from Yorkshire and Lancashire.

Their work was remorselessly hard, regularly difficult and frequently dangerous – but paid significantly more than factory jobs and twice that of land work. Farm labourers might be recruited locally to join the navvies, but were often not considered strong enough. Some navvies were employed directly by the big contractors who undertook whole lines, but more likely they would work for the sub-contractors building sections of the route or be recruited by 'gangers' who led a small team of labourers required for a specific task. Mostly they were employed on a day rate, but sometimes a team would agree a piecework price.

Work on cuttings involved large groups digging out a wide channel through the earth, and then cutting a gully through the rock, filling wagons with the debris, and carting it away by horse back along a temporary line. Alternatively, the navvie attached his filled barrow to a rope and ran the barrow up the side of the incline pulled by a horse – to dump the contents at the top. These barrow runs were inevitably dangerous; in wet weather they were slippery with mud and the load could easily slip off and topple back over the man – particularly if the horse's step broke. Nevertheless, men were expected to move 20 tons a day.

Building embankments broadly reversed this process, with spoil from the cuttings or soil dug from side cuttings laid down along the route, and gradually built up to the right height – the objective being to ensure as small a gradient as possible along the line and the least degree of curve. Trucks loaded with earth and rock were pulled by horses along a temporary rail line to reach the tip-head, where the horses were quickly unhitched and the load dropped over the edge. This too became dangerous when the embankments were high or the weather bad; if there was a slip-up, both men and horses could fall with the load.

Excavating tunnels was undoubtedly the most arduous and dangerous process. Picks were limited in their usefulness and gunpowder had regularly to be used on rock faces. When there was pressure of time or the navvies were tired, serious mistakes were made, and many men were killed or maimed by explosions. Tunnels were often bored by teams working from either end of a hill, and the deepest tunnels also required vertical shafts to be dug down to the level of the line – where the navvies would work in both directions. A pulley and bucket system was used for lowering the men and raising the soil they excavated. As with mining, this was dirty, damp, dangerous employment, worked in 12-hour shifts. And if accidents didn't end their labouring life, their work made them susceptible to dysentery, consumption and lung inflammations.

Wage rates varied during the period in line with the amount of railway building being undertaken at any time, and experienced navvies would tramp to where the money was best. The fortunes of individual navvies varied and some progressed to be sub-contractors. However, all the contractors took financial risks and many went bankrupt, sometimes leaving the navvies unpaid. As the railway building opportunities in Britain ebbed or slowed, many engineers and navvies emigrated to continue their work on the colonial railroads of Canada and Australia, leaving our own lines as a permanent memorial of their stupendous achievement.

A lasting legacy

In the end the impact of the railways in Sussex was more diffuse than the direct physical manifestations of their construction. They promoted social and economic change, encouraged population movement and provided employment. By supplying speedy, reliable transport they enabled the coastal towns to develop as resorts for day-trippers, excursions and holidays, as well as providing a stronger link to the continental ferry services. The numerous links to London from inland towns enabled the rapid transport of fresh produce and encouraged regular business travel and commuting, which in turn grew those towns. The final mark the railways made is seen in the extent of urban growth in the county, a change the pioneers could hardly have imagined.

'SIT ON A SOD & NOD TO ME'

HOW THE VICTORIANS EDUCATED SUSSEX CHILDREN

The changing pattern of educational provision during the period is well reflected by developments in Sussex, in both the public and private spheres, and accurately mirrored the hierarchical structure of Victorian society.

For the majority of Sussex children growing up in rural communities at the time of Victoria's coronation, access to education would have been very limited, and they would most likely have received their 'schooling' at home. Nevertheless, most villages of any size would have had some form of school, even if this were simply a room in the teacher's own home – sometimes referred to as Dame Schools. Dedicated village schools only existed where benefactors – or the established church – provided premises as well as continuing financial support.

Most sponsors were motivated by genuine feelings of benevolence, others by the belief that education was an antidote to social unrest. Those families that could afford to send their children typically paid a contribution of two or three pence each week – thus excluding the poorest villagers – and could expect their child to be taught reading, writing and arithmetic to a basic level. Religious instruction was also always an essential part of the curriculum, and particularly emphasised where the teaching was provided, or supported by, local clergy. In essence all this provision was private and most Sussex children would have had no other formal schooling.

Following initial state incentives in the 1830s, a more coherent system of elementary schools began to develop, run by rival religious organisations of different denominations, including the 'National Society for Promoting the Education of the Poor in the Principles of the Established Church' (the clue to their motive was in the title), which built National Schools, and the nonconformist British and Foreign School Society, which called theirs British Schools. These could obtain state subsidy for buildings from a centralised Committee of Council on Education in exchange for agreeing to keep minimum standards and submit to inspections; in 1840 the Committee issued guidance for the layout of school buildings with oblong schoolrooms and tiered seating that enabled a single schoolteacher to instruct the whole pupil-body at once. The schools were usually small, but would have separate schoolrooms (and entrances) for boys and girls when the numbers justified it. Architects' model designs combined a schoolroom with the teacher's house, and the church authorities favoured the Gothic style because of the morally uplifting ecclesiastical connotations associated with this form. The influential magazine, *The Ecclesiologist*, also declared that a school should be 'the prettiest building in the village, next to the church'.

Village schools

Scores of these schools were built in the county through the middle decades of the century and many of the buildings survive, though often converted to residential or other uses. Nevertheless a good proportion of the original structures are still in use as village schools, usually as Church of England primary schools. Most have naturally been adapted to meet current teaching needs with extensions and additional buildings constructed alongside the originals. However, there are enough surviving examples of village schools for both the architectural form and scholastic character to be still evident today, providing us with a potent image of this aspect of Victorian educational life.

The school in the lovely village of Firle[*], just below the downs, has certainly lasted well. Located at the corner of The Street and Firle Bostal, this is a picturesque building constructed in the typical vernacular style of the area, with a flint-faced walls, red tiles for the roof and red-brick dressings for the windows, door and angles of the walls. The original 1845 schoolroom is a very simple single-storey structure with a central porch, a gable with pierced bargeboards and a hip-knob at the apex. However, the larger part of the building is the two-storey school-teacher's house, complete with its original diamond-pattern windows, set at right angles to the schoolroom and built in the same style.

By contrast, the village school in the High Street at Nutley* is a more substantial building, where the schoolrooms clearly occupy more space than the teacher's accommodation. Although there have been changes to the windows (and an extension at the rear), the form and structure of the building is as it was when it was built in 1853 on land provided by Lord De la Warr. Constructed with a pleasing patch-work of irregularly shaped sandstone blocks, it has a long, red-tiled roof line with a double-height school room set at right angles at one end, visually balanced by the two-storey teacher's house at the other. The latter has an informal mix of features including a pointed-arch doorway, three windows of different shapes and heights, and a bell-cote tucked under one of the gables. The bell may no longer be rung, but after more than 15 decades, this is still a functioning village school.

At Frant*, the school building in the High Street dates from 1852, and is a fairly typical example of the extensively used two-room form. Although front entrances were clearly added later, the original, attractive fretted bargeboards on the gables survive, and there is a canopy below one of them that houses the school bell. An inscription from Proverbs on the façade gives the tone of the teaching: 'Train up a child in the way he should go and when he is Old he will not depart from it.'

Stedham* Primary School, in School Lane, just off the A272, is a charming example of one of the comparatively few rural Board Schools built by local authorities at the end of the century, and is stylistically very different to earlier village schools. From one angle, the building looks more domestic than scholastic, with a large, gently sloping roof with patterned tiling, a prominent chimney, wide dormer windows and decorative tile hanging. In fact, the left-hand section was originally the teacher's accommodation and remains in residential use. Although there has been a ground floor addition at the front, and new buildings at the rear, the stone and brick structure of the attached schoolhouse remains intact, complete with a bell-house projecting from the top of the gable.

The village school at Easebourne* (in Easebourne Street, just off the A272) deserves accolades both for its architecture and the manner in which it has been caringly renovated. Built in 1872 and financed by the local aristocrat, the Earl of Egremont, the wonderfully harmonious design evokes a comforting sense of sanctuary, largely engendered by the materials and details – including warm-coloured, sandstone-rubble walls, bright-red brick dressings, and a series of red-tiled roofs with smart, white-painted, scalloped bargeboards. The plan has the main schoolrooms set at right-angles to each other, with entrance porches at either end, and there is a delightful bell-cote and vane on the hip of the front gable. Although there have been modern additions behind, the original building can be readily appreciated from the street.

A trio of village National Schools over towards the Kent border are still in operation as Church of England primaries. The original part of the Northiam* building (on the A28 Main Street) is of brick with twin pitched roofs over the classrooms. The stone arched doorway and the windows segmented by stone mullions and transoms were typical of the prevalent Victorian revival of medieval and Tudor styles. In this instance the original 1844 building was entirely financed by a local churchman, the Reverend Winser Lord. A substantial addition with large, double-aspect windows dates from 1888 after school attendance became compulsory and the school roll doubled to 260. The somewhat smaller school at Beckley is nearby, going east on the B2088, and is also of brick with stone mullions, though the original glazing has been replaced. Here the two main rooms under pitched roofs are set at right angles to each other and the main entrance, with its own pitched roof, stone arched door and circular window above, juts out to the front of the building. In School Lane, Peasemarsh*, the 1841 school has a rustic simplicity with rubble-stone walls, mullioned windows and a simple two-classroom form – and it retains their use today.

Even where they are no longer used for educational purposes, there are other fine examples of former village schools – in a variety of architectural styles – that are well worth a look.

At Ticehurst*, the red-brick 1846 National School in Church Road was given Grade 2 Listed Building status and has been converted to residential use with original features such as the fretted bargeboards on gable ends – above the windows and front door – retained or restored. There is a simple symmetry in the two-storey design, with two main teaching rooms, and living accommodation on the upper floor. The building was enlarged in 1880 to accommodate the growing number of pupils – following the introduction of compulsory attendance.

The original and visually remarkable school building of 1865 in South Harting*, standing on one side of The Square at the centre of the village, has been almost impeccably conserved. The façade makes a strong visual impact by being faced with light, carefully hewn stone blocks set in regular courses, just like bricks. This contrasts with a pronounced notched pattern of red bricks set around the windows and at the angles of the walls. The composition, with three gables to the front, has further distinctive details including spiky, carved bargeboards that are echoed by similarly spiky crest-tiles, banded tile patterns on the roofs, and windows with lozenge-shaped glazing. What was once a stylish school now provides stylish homes.

Although also now residential, the former National School in Marley Lane, Battle* (just by the entrance to the cemetery), is a striking two-storey design with a façade of three curving, Dutch-style gables with, between them, a pair of arched porches with further gables. In addition there are grey-brick diaper patterns set in the red brickwork, decorative scrollwork above the upper windows and further gables on the side elevations. The architect and school specialist, Henry Kendall junior (1805-85), clearly had ambitions for his design, declaring that 'all materials used in the construction of this building are to be of the best of their respective kind.' As an ill-informed Londoner, he also specified water closets for the 200 children, only to discover that there was no mains water supply in Battle at the time.

The old school at South Street in Falmer[*] has a lovely setting directly opposite the pond. The attractive building of 1837 fits perfectly with the local vernacular style established for this village that formed part of the Egremont estate. At one end there is a schoolroom faced with white flint nodules, lit by a large window with red-brick dressings, and with a gable hung with red tiles; at the other end is a two-storey, bay-windowed teacher's house in matching materials and style. Linking these is a lower range with the smoothly rendered façade and pretty gabled dormers in the long slope of the attic roof. All the detailing, including crest tiles on the hips of the roofs and the finely worked chimneystacks, is very precise.

At Cocking[*], on the A286, a notable and well-preserved former village school can be seen at the corner of Mill Lane. Distinguished by having been designed by Richard Herbert Carpenter (*1841-93*), the architect of Lancing College chapel, it was completed in 1870. It naturally has Gothic windows and door arches, is faced in flint with a red-tiled roof and decorative bargeboards on some of the gables. There was a resident teacher's accommodation at one end, with dormer windows in the upper floor and a distinctive chimneystack with four outlets. Today the whole building is a private residence.

In 1878, another noted Victorian architect, Sir Arthur Blomfield (*1829-99*), produced a splendidly accomplished building in School Lane, Warnham[*], just opposite the village green. Like the other schools discussed here, this combined a schoolhouse with living accommodation, but with the complex, asymmetrical design blending strong shapes with fine details. The façade incorporates three gables, a large schoolroom window divided by stone mullions and transoms, arched stone doorways with drip-moulds and a small tower above the schoolroom door with a pyramidal roof. The walls and prominent chimneystacks are of brick, with extensive tile hanging using both scalloped and straight edged tiles. With windows set at different levels and roofs of different heights at right angles to each other, this adds up to a visually complex but satisfying ensemble. What was once an exceptional village school now provides two exceptional homes.

Ecclesiastically sponsored schools were also built in towns. In Lewes[*], the original Central National Schools' 1843 building in Southover Road, close to the Station Street corner, retains its original form and details — including fretted bargeboards and ornamental dripstone mouldings over the Tudor-style windows. Ruggedly faced in knapped-flint with brick trim, the solidity and symmetry of the two-storey façade gives it very much the flavour of a town institution, rather than a village school.

The library at Bexhill[*], on the corner of Sackville Road and Western Road, is housed in a former school built in 1893. This fine, well-cared-for two-storey building is of red brick, with a dozen sets of Gothic windows set in contrasting stonework. There is a decorative band of moulded brickwork on the façade, and two pairs of windows of the upper floor have brick arches above, topped by pedimented gables. The first floor originally served as the parish room and its form has been retained as the reference library.

The old school at Hailsham[*] is something of a Victorian gem, though its position at the busy intersection of North Street and the High Street — to say nothing of its conversion for use as an Italian restaurant — rather undercuts the village school character. Nevertheless it is an attractive building with many original features including criss-cross patterns in the brickwork, stone surrounds to the windows with pointed Gothic arches to the glazing bars, and a clock-tower surmounted by decorative iron finials. The clock appears to have stopped at three the day the last child left. Many other school buildings of diverse architectural styles and value have survived in varying guises and continue to serve their local communities in different parts of the county. Any list of them would be long, but whether they are now used as meeting halls, community offices, or arts centres, they remain as useful reminders of one aspect of the Victorians' social concerns.

Even where these elementary schools were available, impoverished rural families might be unable to afford the fees and parents might need their children to work with them or care for younger siblings. By the age of ten, children would be considered ready to earn wages. In the towns, child labour was common and again families would be reluctant to lose a child's minimal earnings in order to send them to school. For the already educated and wealthy classes, the conditions were different. Private education could, of course, be bought; richer families could employ individual tutors or governesses and fee-paying schools were readily available for boys, either as boarders or in their hometown. The old Grammar Schools offered a limited alternative for a chosen few in larger towns. Thus all education was voluntary, haphazard in provision and privately provided.

The state steps in

However, reforms during the 19th century slowly began to usher in a period of government involvement. An Act of 1834 required Poor Law Unions to provide for the education of the children in the workhouses, in effect creating the first state schools. From 1833 The Factory Acts not only limited the hours of child labour, but introduced some minimal schooling on the premises. A system of 'payment by results' introduced by the government in 1862 required the elementary schools to prepare children for examination in the three Rs in order to determine the level of state support – and obliged parents to ensure their childrens' daily attendance. However, bad weather, epidemics and the demands for hands during the Sussex hop harvest undermined the scheme.

With countless children still not being schooled, and the captains of Victorian commerce requiring a more literate workforce, the big change came with the Education Act of 1870 which required public money for the establishment of state elementary schools in areas where provision was inadequate. Locally elected School Boards built and maintained new schools for the children of their area aged between 5 and 13. For many years fees were payable (up to three times the rate for voluntary schools) by all but the poorest, and by 1880 attendance was compulsory, with 'Board Men' enforcing the rule by dealing with truancy, but it was not until 1891 that most elementary schools abolished fees. Many of these non-denominational Board Schools were established in Sussex, mostly in the larger towns, and some of their buildings survive today.

Of the 19 that were built in Brighton*, the surviving Board Schools provide good examples of the genre, particularly where the buildings are still fully functional schools. The architectural approach was novel, and adopted styles that had been promoted in London and other cities. As secular authorities, the School Boards were able to turn away from the ecclesiastically imbued Gothic style as being inappropriate; instead architects searched other historical precedents for inspiration, giving some of the buildings a flavour identified as neo-Queen Anne style – characterised by the use of red brick, classically shaped sash windows with white glazing bars, variously-shaped gables and asymmetrical compositions. Because of the cost of urban land and the need to accommodate large numbers of children, the designers built upwards – typically producing triple-decker buildings. Changes in educational practice also required the inclusion of smaller classrooms for different age groups, as well as large schoolrooms.

The form of the Elm Grove School (just between the Wellington Street and Bonchurch Road turnings) stands as a good example, if one ignores the later additions. Built on a sloping site, the composite structure has some smaller classroom windows at five different levels and other large, double-height schoolroom windows. There is great visual variety in the detail, with different brick colours used for banding and window dressings, some decorative terracotta mouldings and stonework adding emphasis to the gables. With red-tiled roofs of different shapes and heights, a variety of gable shapes, prominent chimneys and two cupolas, the building has a lively skyline. Elm Grove was completed in 1893, and like other Board Schools from that period was intended to serve a local working-class population, offering an educational beacon to underprivileged children – in this case almost in the shadow of the local workhouse just up the hill.

However, the most impressive and best maintained of these buildings is probably St Luke's School, which fronts Queen's Park Rise and St Luke's Terrace. Although not completed till 1903, this architecturally striking edifice still exemplifies the late Victorian spirit of educational progress. Harmonious, rather than simply symmetrical in elevation, the triple-decker building sits boldly astride the rising land and is composed

Victorian teaching methods

Village schools were small-sized in relation to the numbers; initial plans allowed just six square feet (just over half a square metre) per pupil (a third of the minimum allowed nowadays), so benches or desks were tightly packed. At first teachers were unqualified, poorly paid and largely from the same labouring class as their pupils. They were responsible for covering just reading, writing and arithmetic, sometimes also scripture. Being able to read passages from the bible was the test of literacy. Where there was only one teacher, lessons might be given to the whole school; learning by rote was a standard method. Discipline was the natural corollary of controlling large numbers; the cane and dunce's cap were basic items. Groups were mixed in age and ability, although often separated by gender – either with segregated rooms or a dividing partition in the classroom. Equipment was limited to sand boxes or slates for the children to practise writing, and a blackboard for the teacher. Books were restricted in number and often shared. The school day was divided into two three-hour sessions with a two-hour break for children to return home – perhaps walking some distance – for midday meals.

From around the mid-century the Church of England started training teachers and a system of apprentice pupil-teachers was introduced for 'children' as young as 13. The Board Schools in towns also adopted a monitorial system for coping with large numbers; this involved teachers relaying lessons to the youngest pupils through older pupil-monitors. Thus infants would learn from standard reading cards like this, well, frankly, odd one:

Sit on a sod and nod to me. A cat sits on a sod and nods to the lad.
A lad sits on a sod and nods to a cat and to me. It is not a sin to sit
on a sod. Am I to sit on a sod and nod? No.

History and geography were added to the syllabus, though these mostly involved learning sequences of dates or names. Grammar might be taught, but writing was about copying, not composition. Nevertheless, these schools and systems saw out the Victorian period till they were replaced by the Local Education Authorities in 1902.

of strong forms, including a projecting central block with large windows on two floors, a pair of towers rising above the roof line, topped with lanterns capped by cupolas, and a further lantern feature on the ridge of the roof. There is boldness in the façade too; strong bands of stucco contrast with the mixture of red and grey brickwork; a stucco cornice below the parapet is marked by a tooth pattern; and a jolly variety of window shapes and sizes. Other enlivening details include patches of herringbone pattern brickwork, banded chimneystacks and the School Board's own insignia prominently displayed within a wide arch. Not simply a school, this is a citadel of teaching, trumpeting the Victorian's faith in the transformative power of education and a monument to one of the achievements of the age – free education.

Public means private

The other major educational development that characterised the Victorian period, was the significant growth of fee-paying 'public' schools. The demand for these originated with the burgeoning middle-classes who saw the advantages of equipping their sons for dealing with new demands of the age. Admission to the civil service and army was by competitive examination; lawyers, like doctors, had to achieve professional requirements; a good education gave access to the newer professions such as engineering and surveying. The aspirations of the middle-class also focused on manners and social advancement; the right education could lubricate the hinges that opened the doors of opportunity. Public schools offered to teach Christian morality, leadership and self-reliance; qualities central to the Victorian value system.

The ideal location for establishing new public schools required space for buildings and playing fields, a rural position and access to the railway system that would bring boarders to school. Sussex offered all these, and an enterprising educational propagandist and Sussex curate called Nathaniel Woodward established three of his many independent colleges in the county with the aim of achieving 'the union of classes by a common system of education' – although in the end the fee-paying schools mostly served the interests of a clientele from a limited, middle-class strata of society. All three survive today as testimony to the continuing appeal of this Victorian educational ideal.

St John's College, just outside Hurstpierpoint* can be seen from College Lane. It was designed by Richard Cromwell Carpenter (*1812-55*) and started use in 1853. Built in the Gothic mode using traditional Sussex knapped flint, the exterior of the buildings are rather gaunt, though the interior quadrangle with the original hall and chapel (designed by Carpenter's son and completed in 1865) is more inviting. The grounds of the College are private and access is naturally limited by school activities. However, visitors wanting to get a closer look at the buildings can phone 01273 833636 in advance to ask when access might be possible.

Lancing* College was also designed by Richard Cromwell Carpenter, although he died before it opened in 1858. The three-storey quadrangle with cloisters on three sides is in the Gothic style, built with knapped flints with stone dressings and quoins. There are later parts designed by other hands, including Carpenter's partner William Slater, and his son Richard Herbert Carpenter – whose outstanding contribution is the impressive Gothic Revival Chapel noted on page 15. The school complex, which sits above the River Adur just off the A27, is not open to the public, but visitors to the chapel get a good view of the main buildings.

Ardingly* College (on College Road, just outside the village) was also designed by Slater with the younger Carpenter, and completed in 1870. Built in red brick in the Gothic style, it is arranged around two large open-ended courtyards separated by a block containing a dining hall and library with, at one end, a chapel completed in 1883. Although not particularly inspiring, the ensemble of buildings has a very fine setting, is surrounded by extensive playing fields and offers splendid rural views. The buildings can be seen from College Road, but there is also a public right of way through the site from the main gates. Visitors wanting to see more should make arrangements with the school office in advance by telephoning 01444 893000.

Historically, Woodward's schools were predated by the establishment in 1845 of Brighton* College by William Aldwin Soames and a group of local worthies, as Sussex's first public school. The College has a large site that includes playing fields, and buildings from different periods. The main façade is a set of strikingly distinctive Gothic Revival buildings on Eastern Road, opposite the College Road turning. This range, designed by distinguished Old Brightonian Thomas Graham Jackson (*1835-1924*) and completed in 1887, is a three and four-storey block in red brick. The numerous pointed windows are dressed in moulded terracotta, with elaborate tracery and floral ornaments, and there are patterns of knapped flint set into the brickwork, as well as moulded tiles depicting leaping dolphins. The double-arched gatehouse is particularly flamboyant, being decorated with white moulded tiles in ornamental patterns above the arches and with florid designs above the windows.

Inside the grounds are earlier buildings, including a chapel, designed by George Gilbert Scott (*1811-78*) and completed in 1859. Although Gothic in style, these are different in flavour, being built in flint with stone dressings. There is no public access to these, and the buildings can only be glimpsed from the surrounding streets.

Eastbourne[*] too acquired a public school with the college founded in 1867 by the seventh Duke of Devonshire and other prominent local citizens. This is a large site, with an attractive expanse of playing fields, is located between College Road and Grange Road, not far from the town centre and the sea. There is a mix of red-brick Gothic- and Tudor-style buildings on the campus, with some dating from the 20th century. The original Victorian buildings face Blackwater Road and were designed by Henry Currey (*1821-1900*), the Duke's regular architect. They consist of the red-brick School House, to which a façade with two castellated towers and a wide-arched entrance were added in 1901; a second building to its right also with stone-dressed Tudor-style windows; and a red-brick chapel on the corner of College Road with Gothic windows and doors. The overall effect of the architecture is certainly studied and serious; this could only really be a 'public' school.

And finally, the girls

So Sussex boys from well-to-do families, and others sent from further afield, did pretty well from all this local provision. However, their sisters, despite years of agitation by female emancipationists, had to wait longer before top-of-the-range schooling was available for them. An Act of 1869 had prevented endowed schools from restricting entry to boys and was intended to encourage the creation of girls' schools, but it was not until 1885 that the three Lawrence sisters established what became Roedean School for girls in Brighton[*]. The building dating from 1898 that you can see today on the downs above Marine Drive (the coastal A259) is 150 metres wide, and contained both the school and dormitories; it looks rather forbidding, and public access is not possible.

The other important Sussex institutions associated with female education were the Diocesan training colleges for schoolmistresses, and two of their buildings remain. The one established in Brighton[*] in 1854 and extended in 1886, survives as the Brighton Business Centre on the corner of Ditchling Road and Viaduct Road. Designed in the Gothic Revival style, its central section and two long wings are faced in knapped flint, with stone dressings, grey-brick quoins and a slate covered roof – in effect, all tones of grey. The other building is the Bishop Otter College in Chichester[*]. Although originally established to train masters in the Diocese, in 1873, following a campaign by the formidable Louisa Hubbard (*1836-1905*) to encourage the acceptance of women as teachers, it became exclusively a training college for women – and kept the single-sex regime till 1957. Although now part of the University of Chichester campus, the original building in College Lane dating from 1850 is a sombre, somewhat stolid edifice. The style – broadly medieval monastic – and substance – dark stone under a grey slate roof – probably accurately reflected Victorian attitudes to its original worthy purpose. There is a long façade overlooking a neat lawn, an integral chapel in one wing and a bell-cote with weathervane on the roof as the sole light touch.

Specialist schools

By the last quarter of the century, the broadening of the educational canvas covered various specialist schools and colleges. In 1874 Lewes[*] acquired a School of Art and Science, and this listed building survives today on the corner of Albion Street and East Street, having served for some years as the town library. Designed by the County Surveyor, Henry Card, not surprisingly it is in the prevalent Gothic style – in this case in red brick with pointed window arches accentuated by contrasting white and grey bricks, together with a central entrance porch with a pointed stone arch and a little parapet above. The façade is symmetrical, and the square plan of the building is reinforced by a pair of steeply pitched pavilion roofs at each corner, topped by platforms with cast-iron balustrades and weather-vane finials. A pair of wrought-iron lamps on the entrance steps was added to mark Victoria's Diamond Jubilee in 1897. To modern eyes, the building looks quaintly small, but this undoubtedly reflects the state of specialist higher education in the town at the time it was built. Today it just provides enough space for the resident architectural practice.

Brighton's* Municipal Technical College on Richmond Terrace was designed by the Borough Surveyor and Engineer, Francis May. The original, and most noteworthy, central section of the redbrick and terracotta building was completed in 1896; it comprised two bays of three stories either side of a central section, rising higher to a shaped gable crowned by a triangular pediment and flanked by octagonal piers with decorative cornices. Sympathetically designed extensions on both sides were added at later dates and the building has recently been converted to apartments, with the renovation of the façade emphasising the special value of the terracotta materials. Terracotta tiles are used across the ground-floor façade, as surrounds for the windows and for the cornices.

However, it is the extensive use of moulded terracotta for decoration that gives the building its special character. These include pediments above windows and decorations high in the gable, but the most fanciful usage can be seen at ground level where the terracotta-capped front wall has elaborately moulded tops to the piers. Terracotta was practical as a facing material – its hard surface resisted damp and pollution – and fashionable, making this very much a building of its time. In the evening sunlight, it still glows appropriately with the spirit of Victorian technical innovation.

SERVING THE PEOPLE

CIVIC BUILDINGS FOR A CIVIL SOCIETY

A s a result of reformist campaigns and political struggle, the Victorian period witnessed important advances in the democratic processes – together with significant changes in the structure of local government. Although these changes were concerned with improving the organisation and administration of local services, the developments found natural expression in the construction of a number of significant Victorian buildings in Sussex that survive today, and declare visibly the values of civic pride and community aspiration.

Change was certainly overdue. Before the mid-1830s there was no consistent pattern of district administration that we would recognise as local government. Instead there was an unco-ordinated hotchpotch of bodies with authority and power, often inefficient or indolent, frequently corrupt or partisan, usually undemocratic or arbitrary with the use of their power – and some with histories dating back to medieval times. Counties had the powerful Quarter Sessions of landed Justices of the Peace – in a real sense, the rural ruling class – empowered to levy rates on the parishes and responsible for bridges, roads, militia, police, prisons, coroners, and administering the Poor Law – as well as dispensing justice.

Locally each parish had its controlling vestry, typically dominated by the clergy, larger farmers and the wealthier parishioners, with a discriminatory franchise of house-holding ratepayers – those paying rates on larger properties being allocated more votes. Mostly its concerns were pragmatic and small-scale; the upkeep of the church, repairing parish roads and cutting hedges. But they were also responsible for the local administration of the Poor Law, with plenty of leeway as to how they dealt with the paupers of the parish.

Then there were the municipal corporations, each with their own royal charter, constitution and history. These were the old market and trading towns with rights to representation in the House of Commons, but with an electorate restricted to corporation members. These privileges politicised their role, and laid them open to corruption, as well as tending to distract them from attending to their responsibilities for water supplies, drainage and street cleaning.

Finally, there were a large number of formally constituted bodies created to serve special purposes and with their own specific powers. These included Turnpike Trusts, Drainage Boards and town Improvement or Paving Commissioners.

From corruption to incorporation

The impact of the industrial revolution in creating new industrial towns that didn't fit into these archaic patterns, together with the extension of the parliamentary franchise following the Reform Bill of 1832, produced the impetus for further change with the passing of the Municipal Corporations Act of 1835, which swept away the old closed corporations. The act, as the name suggests, was primarily aimed at the larger towns and industrial cities with populations of over 22,000. However, the legislation was significant in giving the vote to all male ratepayers (home-owners, that is), and in creating elected councils with aldermen, a mayor and paid officers. Once individual towns had obtained corporation status, the councils were required to form a police force and allowed to make social improvements – though many were slow to achieve this.

For all of the century up until 1854, Brighton[*] had been administered by a group of unelected vestrymen, together with the more accountable Improvement Commissioners – the latter responsible for paving, cleaning and lighting the streets and running the market. Once the town obtained its first charter of incorporation, control passed to the elected council, and the administration grew as it took on new responsibilities including public health, water supply and sewerage. However, even before its official incorporation Brighton had its own multi-purpose town hall, built in 1832, where the commissioners met, concerts were held and the police had their headquarters. This is the Greek Revival-style building with porticos that stands in Bartholomew Square and that became officially known as the Town Hall. Although pre-Victorian in origin, the building was substantially remodelled at the end of the 19th century to suit the increased needs of the borough, including adding a notable freestanding staircase and galleries to the first floor offices. The Council Chamber is on the second floor and there are still the original police holding cells in the basement.

The new town halls

Further administrative reform and local democratisation came with the 1888 Local Government Act, which established elected County Councils and formally divided Sussex into two parts, East Sussex and West Sussex. An additional act of 1894 completed the organisational process by creating a pattern of new Urban, Rural and local Borough Councils as well as formalising parish councils.

Some of these councils made use of existing buildings – Chichester[*] already had its own Council Chambers from the 18th century – or did not require new buildings immediately. Horsham found an odd compromise by rebuilding its existing town hall in 1888. The building in Market Square retained the original façade from the building the Duke of Norfolk had erected in 1812, complete with regal, ducal and civic arms carved in three panels. Behind this the two-storey Victorian structure is less distinctive, but with a series of round arched windows that echo the form of the front door and the blind arcades either side of it. Either way, you can certainly see the join between the parts – despite the similarity of the stone colours.

Other Sussex towns built new town halls in different styles. Perhaps the grandest statement of newly found civic substance can be found in

*Eastbourne[1], on the corner of Grove Road and Saffrons Road. Designed by the competition-winning Birmingham architect W. Tadman-Faulkes, this substantial and very costly building took two years to complete and was opened in 1886. Built primarily of red brick with Portland stone dressings and a slate roof, it is usually described as being in the Free Renaissance style, though the disconcerting blend of features suggests the range of influences on Victorian architects and the taste of the council-lors commissioning the building. The three-storey façade is assertively asymmetrical, with an over-high clock tower set to the left of centre, and the two pavilion-like projections of distinctly different widths at either end of the frontage. There is the predictable formal projecting portico covering the steps to the street, supported by four stone piers. Above this are a balcony with a balustrade, decorative urns and a stone shield with the town crest carved in high relief. All the usual elements of Victorian municipal aspiration are there, even if imperfectly expressed.

The town hall in *Bexhill[2] is smaller, but still clearly a civic building of the same period, having been built immediately after the creation of the town's new Urban District Council. Designed by Henry Ward (*1854-1927*) and dated 1894, it stands by the end of the London Road overlooking a small garden (designated Town Hall Square), the centre-piece of which is a quintessential piece of Victoriana – an over-elaborated memorial dedicated to the council's first chairman. The neat-looking building itself is of red brick with horizontal bands of stone emphasis-ing the three stories. The main entrance is also of smoothly finished stone, its stab at classical prominence being expressed by the use of paired columns on either side of an arch, with a stone balustrade above. Two slightly projecting wings have strongly defined windows on the first floor, further balustrades on the second level and the façade's com-position is topped off with four jolly cupolas crowning small turrets to either side of the gables. Alongside the main structure is a companion

---

1. *Eastbourne: for dates of meetings in the Council Chamber, contact 01323 410000 or www.eastbourne.gov.uk/council.*
2. *Bexhill: for dates of meetings in the Council Chamber, contact 01424 787813 or www.rother.gov.uk/committees.*

section containing the council chamber itself. The façade of this is given distinction by a large, classically inspired first floor balcony – featuring an arch, columns and a balustrade – and with a stone-capped pediment above. One imagines this was thought to be the perfect platform for a town official addressing crowds or announcing election results.

By contrast, the Victorian town hall in *Hastings[3] is a distinctly heavyweight affair, even if the frontage on Queen's Road is modestly narrow. Built in 1880, and also designed by Henry Ward in an Early English Gothic style, it sits on a triangular site bounded by Queen's Square and Station Road. The appearance of heaviness comes from the use of roughish stone rubble combined with a similar tone of the smoother ashlar dressings around windows and doors, giving the building an almost monochromatic look. That said, the Queen's Road façade is visually vigorous, if a little pompous; the central arched entrance incorporates triple granite colonettes on either side with a large stone balcony above, and the first floor features three pairs of tall windows, again with granite colonettes, and a rose window below a central pediment. All the first-floor windows have stained glass, conferring an ecclesiastical tone, though in fact the designs are shields and floral motifs. The side of the building has a first-floor bay to the Council Chamber, again with similar features to the façade, and a bell-cote to the right of the elaborately formed pediment. Next to this is a sequence of four three-storey bays with, between the second and third floor windows, a series of carved stone panels depicting historical incidents associated with Hastings. The Council Chamber itself has a baronial-style fireplace, griffins, tiling and panelling, as well as an arch-braced roof

The town hall in *Arundel[4], close to the High Street end of marvellous Maltravers Street, is stern, even forbidding, but nevertheless noteworthy. Its solidly defensive character probably owes something to

---

3. *Hastings: for access dates contact the Information Centre on 0845 274 1001 or via www.hastings.gov.uk.*

4. *Arundel: readers wanting to see the interior of the building should contact the Town Hall in advance on 01903 882954; their operating hours are limited to 10.00 to 12.30 weekdays except Wednesday.*

its genesis, having been provided by the local Duke of Norfolk in exchange for the town ceding land for him to extend his nearby castle. An early example of a council negotiating 'planning gain', it seems. In keeping with the Duke's own premises, his architect produced a bastion-like edifice in dark knapped flint with two flanking towers. These are topped by jutting parapets with pseudo machicolations – the openings that defenders used for dropping missiles and boiling liquids when under attack. However, the ground floor is more approachable, with a three-arch logia constructed in Pulborough stone, designed in the Norman style, and with a parapet above. Three round-arched windows on the first floor echo the form, and above them is the coat of arms of the borough together with the Howard lion and Fitzalan horse. The whole project took a few years to complete, but the Council Chamber was in use by 1838.

Access to Council Chambers

Town Hall interiors and their Council Chambers are usually only accessible when there are Council or other meetings open to the public. Where access is possible, we have included contact details in footnotes for readers wishing to check dates in advance of a visit.

The unabashedly red-brick town hall in Lewes[*], designed by the Brighton architect Samuel Denman and dating from 1893, fits neatly into the High Street, close to the crest of the hill. This is a bold design, full of visual interest and drawing on a number of architectural styles for inspiration. The moulded-brick façade stands on a contrasting well-scrubbed stone plinth, and rises to three storeys, with the parapet above lightened by sets of blind arches. Despite not being symmetrical, and with a projecting section rising above the main door, the building has a comfortable solidity – probably aided by the classical proportions of the windows and the strong horizontal lines in the façade. The arched entrance doors and two of the ground-floor windows are strikingly enlivened by alternate segments of stone and brick, with classical heads carved into the keystones. There are many other incidental details to note, including plenty of terracotta designs and decorations, some of the original metalwork and the town crest carved in terracotta below the topmost pediment. Although the interior is not generally open to the public, a notable Elizabethan staircase can be seen inside the main entrance when the building is in use.

Community buildings and public benefactors

Lewes has other Victorian buildings erected to serve the local population. Further along the High Street, near Westgate Street, is the notable Freemasons' Hall, built in 1868. This is broadly in the Gothic Revival style, but more particularly the Venetian variation that the influential critic John Ruskin promoted through his researches and writing about Venice. So here, what might have been a bland edifice, is a light-coloured brick façade brightened with bands and patterns using a mixture of red brick, terracotta and grey tiles. The cheery effect is further enhanced by dark foliage designs cut into the stonework and a pair of barley-twist drainpipes. This is no canal-side palazzo, but nevertheless provides a nice contrast in a Sussex high street.

The Venetian theme continues in a stronger vein with another of Lewes's Victorian community buildings, the remarkable Fitzroy Memorial Library that stands on Friar's Walk, just at the edge of the pedestrian area that leads to the bridge over the Ouse. Indeed, one has the sense that had this been set up a few hundred metres away at the water's edge, the Venice conceit might have been more successful. As it stands, this would be a striking building in any context. Built in 1862 by the widow of the Lewes MP Henry Fitzroy (public patronage allied with private grief), it was designed by no less an architectural luminary than Sir George Gilbert Scott (1811-78), whose firm's other work included the Foreign Office in Whitehall, the Midland Grand Hotel, St Pancras and the Albert Memorial in London. Constructed in rather un-Venetian red brick, the façade nevertheless resembles a small palazzo, with a pointed-arch door surround and marble columns surmounted by a balcony with decorative iron railings. Above this the first-floor window rises in a prominent arch above the cornice level, and there are four pairs of smaller Italian Gothic windows also featuring marble columns with carefully carved foliage capitals. The slate hipped roof, with decorative crest-tiles and delicate finials, is crowned by a clock housing, itself topped with a dainty spire. Now a private residence known as Fitzroy House, and only open on special occasions, it is still a building for any town to relish.

Hastings[*] also benefited from the largesse of its local parliamentarian, and was provided with the Brassey Institute in Claremont, off Robertson Street, given to the town by Lord Brassey in 1887, just after he retired as their Member of Parliament. This seems a quintessential Victorian building, both in terms of its characteristic architecture and its function in providing broadly educational facilities for the community – including a reference library on the ground floor, an assembly room on the first floor and a school of art and science on the upper floors. The gift seems a generous act of patronage, but it must be remembered that Brassey's father, the first Thomas Brassey, had been one of the country's leading railway contractors who built about a sixth of the nation's rail network; naturally when he died he left a huge fortune.

The building, designed by W.L. Vernon, is essentially Gothic Revival in style, though really rather fanciful in execution and detail. Seemingly squeezed into a tight town-centre site, it is four storeys high with a tower and truncated spire rising higher. The façade of each floor is treated very differently, giving the building both vivacity and visual interest. The ground-floor windows, including a bay, are divided by mullions and transoms; the first floor has two recessed windows with arches and a central bay with a pointed arch and geometrical tracery; on the third floor there is a pretty arcaded loggia with the windows set back, and the top floor has three simpler windows. The tower section with an arched doorway has the windows mostly offset from the height of the others and again of different designs, including one with a balcony. The whole effect is enriched with decorative panels, mouldings and a mix of materials. In other words, this is a bit of architectural indulgence, but achieved with some aplomb. You need to stand back to fully appreciate the façade and to take in the interesting adjoining buildings including, to the right, the *Observer* and *Advertiser* Offices, designed by the same architect, which feature a wide, timber-framed window projecting from the third floor and painted panels depicting printing processes. Given the Institute's origins, it seems entirely appropriate that it now serves as Hasting's main library, also making it possible for much of the interior to be seen.

Another Sussex benefactor, the philanthropist and enthusiastic promoter of homeopathy, William Leaf (*1791-1874*), provided Eastbourne[*] with a Working Men's Hall on Seaside, close to the Burfield Road turning. The 1863 foundation stone makes his rather patronising intentions clear '…to promote the social and moral and spiritual welfare of the working classes of Eastbourne' – though this was probably code for temperance. The neo-Gothic style and somewhat ecclesiastical tenor of the building reinforce his intentions, though a certain architectural quirkiness adds a touch of cheer. The main part of the brick-built building has a first-floor hall with a set of five pointed-arch windows set in stone, with a further round window contained within an arch-shape moulding. The ground-floor windows are characterised by columns with floral capitals and arches formed with multi-coloured bricks. The big feature, though, is a corner tower with the main door set in an elaborate stone surround and, above, three storeys of windows all with more polychromatic brickwork, the whole topped off with a steeple containing four prominent clock faces.

Housing the police and prisoners

Alongside the Victorian reforms in local government, came a determined effort to improve policing in the country and to establish fully accountable professional forces. Hitherto, villages had relied on individual constables, whilst the towns had various *ad hoc* arrangements for policing with Watchmen under the direction of the local Justices. Even after reforms in the 1830s encouraging the formation of town and county forces, progress was generally slow. Chichester established a small force from 1836, though constables were initially part-timers. Brighton's force started in 1838 and grew to 60 officers by 1854 to police a population of 46,000. East Sussex established a force from 1840 based in Framfield, in the Chief Constable's own home, whilst Hastings based its 9 officers in the old town hall. After 1856 it became mandatory for the counties and boroughs to have their own police establishment, partly financed and inspected by central government, and the West Sussex Constabulary was set up in 1857 at Petworth. In time they all built their own police stations, and a few of these survive today as witness to this aspect of Victorian civil society.

The original County Police Station in Battle[*] (situated next to the roundabout between the A2100 London Road and A271 North Trade Road) is still partly in use by the police. The pair of neatly utilitarian buildings dating from 1861 is of grey brick, with contrasting red-brick dressings around the arched windows and prominent red-brick quoins at the corners of the building. What appear to be the original lamp housing and decorative wrought-iron supports over the entrance gateway, have survived intact. When built, the station was the base for a superintendent, two sergeants and 12 constables and there was also space for a small Petty Sessions Court.

Though now converted to office and residential use, the Police Station at Hurst Green[*] was combined with a smart-looking Court House. Situated on London Road, the 1892 buildings face the end of Station Road and appear somewhat unusual, perhaps readily being mistaken for a schoolroom or village hall. The simple, single-storey red-brick Court House is small, but nevertheless sober – the heavier stone dressings, central clock-tower, bell-cote and cupola, together with the carved armorial shield, giving it a certain gravitas. The attached Police House is blander, but stylistically of a piece with the Court House, which also contained a small cell wing.

Lewes[*] has its Victorian Police Station in West Street. Not a particularly distinguished building, it has more of a Georgian flavour about it, with white-painted sash windows and a main door set in deeply grooved ashlar. Just two stories high, it has gables above the two projecting bays and slate tiles on the roof. Whatever its visual limitations, the building, and the adjacent 1905 extension, still serve the original purpose.

Lewes's more significant and substantial edifice representing the Victorian forces of law and order is the prison on the A227 Brighton

Road, close to the corner with Nevill Road. Not surprisingly this is a dour, fortress-like structure made even more sombre by being faced in dark, knapped flint. The façade, completed in 1853 and designed by a Birmingham architect D.R. Hill, consists of four heavy towers with projecting parapets at the top, and round-arched windows dressed in brick or stone at three levels. There is a high, wide arch for the main entrance and the only more human element is the Governor's House set to one side – but still in the same gaunt style.

Many of the prisoners bound for a spell at Lewes Prison will have passed through the former County Courthouse building at 118 Church Street, Brighton*, sited just opposite The Dome. Despite its fundamental function, there is nothing overbearing about this fine building. Just two stories high in red brick with a modest frontage and an asymmetrical façade, it has Gothic Revival windows set in stone surrounds with sloping sills and a curious lone buttress with angled stone caps. The chief feature is the Judge's Entrance set in a stone projection, with a pointed arch, ornamental bands and a crenellated top. A further archway to the side of the building, with the County Court inscription and a panel containing the Royal Arms carved in relief, leads to the original public entrance. As the only Victorian building of its kind in the county, the fabric and its original interior features are worthy of care and preservation.

Villages were inevitably too small to justify the building of special police stations and the local constables found their accommodation where they could. However, at Rotherfield* there are a couple of red-brick Eridge Estate cottages dated 1889, which served as the police house. The pair, in South Street, is recognisable by the porches, the decorative row of terracotta roses, and the Abergavenny crest on the façade. The police notice board was fixed to the wall below the crest.

Thus by the end of the period, the Victorians had established the principles and much of the structure of local administration that we have inherited. Even if boundaries have been redrawn and areas re-designated, the underlying functions owe a great deal to their initiatives.

VICTORIAN TREATMENTS

HOW SUSSEX COPED WITH THE SICK, THE MAD & THE DEAD

The Victorian period saw significant and substantial changes in medical knowledge and practice, together with the growth and establishment of a variety of institutions for treating the physically unwell and the mentally unstable. These included voluntary hospitals, dispensaries, cottage hospitals, workhouse infirmaries, asylums, specialist hospitals, isolation hospitals for infectious diseases, sanatoria, convalescent homes and, eventually, general hospitals. Various examples of what was built in the county remain in some form today, allowing us to trace the impact of the Victorian approach to the treatment of illnesses in the buildings they produced, all of which are of historical interest and some of architectural note.

At the start of the Victorian period only charitable hospitals existed, financed by initial bequests and maintained by donations and public subscriptions. These voluntary hospitals could only really flourish where there was a large enough population to sustain them, so patients might have to travel substantial distances for hospital treatment. Chichester[*] had the Royal West Sussex Hospital established in 1828; although pre-Victorian, it served the town throughout the period. This wide-fronted and stuccoed building in Broyle Road survives today as Forbes Place, converted into a set of elegant apartments that form part of a larger residential enclave just outside the city centre. Likewise Brighton[*] had already established the Royal Sussex County Hospital in 1828, which still operates today in Eastern Road. Designed by Sir Charles Barry (*1795-1860*), who later designed the Houses of Parliament in a very different manner, the original part of the cream stucco-fronted building is in the classical style with a triangular pediment over the central projecting section, prominent cornices on the wings and carefully proportioned windows. Further wings were added during Victoria's reign, including one commemorating her golden jubilee, and a separate outpatients department was established in 1896 in a small, but much altered building across the road.

Initially voluntary hospital patients required a letter of recommendation from a benefactor or subscriber to receive treatment, but later patients simply turned up for admission, though they might be challenged about their income. Otherwise any Victorian who could afford it would pay for a doctor to treat him or her in their home, including the supervision of childbirth or even surgery. Doctors worked in the voluntary hospitals without payment to gain valuable experience, and to establish a reputation with the local subscribers and patrons – their potential clientele. These hospitals were in essence general hospitals, dealing with accidents and injuries, and attempting to treat a range of commonly recognised illnesses and diseases, and usually with an outpatients department. However, admissions policies excluded incurables, patients with chronic conditions or infectious diseases, and the mentally ill – for whom other provision might be available. Larger towns might also have a Public Dispensary providing free medicine, advice and treatment to the labouring classes

The poorest ill and infirm, and those excluded by the voluntary hospitals, would most likely find themselves in the local Union workhouse (*see p.23*). These workhouses had originally been intended to serve the impoverished able-bodied, but in time found themselves providing increasingly for those whose poverty was caused by illness, but in conditions that were appalling. Following the publication of critical reports and consequent legislative changes in 1867, the Boards of Guardians of the larger workhouses, such as Horsham, Chailey and Cuckfield, eventually erected separate Union infirmaries for treating their sick. In due course these also treated other poor patients from the locality, and by the end of the century their role eclipsed that of the voluntary hospitals, in effect making the Union infirmaries early state hospitals. Even after the workhouses closed, these sometimes bleak-looking infirmaries continued to operate as hospitals for a time. The Brighton* Workhouse established its first Infirmary in 1866, further medical blocks were erected there by the end of the century and the whole Workhouse eventually became the Brighton General Hospital.

Containing epidemics

For Victorians, the medical scares and scourges of the time all revolved around epidemics. The most devastating of these was cholera, which was mistakenly believed to be contagious, until proven in the 1840s to be water-borne. However, contagious diseases such as scarlet fever – which accounted for one in 20 deaths – smallpox, measles or diphtheria were also prevalent in most cities and towns, where the tightly packed population was always readily susceptible to infection whenever there was an outbreak. Although by its rural nature Sussex was less prone to widespread contagion, there were significant mid-century epidemics in Chichester and Brighton and a cholera epidemic in Hastings in 1849. But it was the horrendous metropolitan experiences and panics that raised public awareness, and precipitated political action aimed at restricting the impact of outbreaks of infection through the creation of isolation hospitals. As usual it was the poor who copped it worst, so in Sussex it was mainly the Union workhouses who found it necessary to provide isolation wards or separate buildings, though voluntary hospitals could find themselves dealing with similar patients. Meanwhile it became the responsibility of the sanitary authorities for dealing with infectious diseases and to provide isolation hospitals; an Act of 1889 made notification of infectious diseases mandatory. The Brighton Workhouse had a fever block in its grounds, and in addition the town established a Borough Sanatorium and Infectious Diseases Hospital away from the city centre in Bevendean Road. Burgess Hill was served by an isolation hospital at Goddard's Green and there was one at Newhaven.

In 1889, Eastbourne* built an infectious diseases hospital, the Borough Sanatorium, that later became known as Downside Hospital. Significantly this stood isolated at the edge of the Old Town area, and away from the centres of the town's growing population. Initially it dealt with infections like scarlet fever and diphtheria, but in time the hospital grew into a substantial complex dealing with a range of diseases. Most of the site has been redeveloped for residential uses, although the original nurses' home and some other accommodation survives. Now in private residential use as Downside Court, the building can be seen from the roadside in East Dean Road on the hill leading to the open Downs, close to the turning for Cherry Garden Road.

This is a comfortingly domestic-looking building, conforming to the residential architectural style of the time – three storeys high, with steep pitched roofs and gables to the front, bay windows on the ground floor and much attractive tile-hanging on the upper floors. An archway through to the rear led to stables – as well as to a small mortuary. More typical for Sussex though, were the cottage hospitals, sanatoria and convalescent homes that were built throughout the county.

Cottage hospitals and convalescent homes

Cottage hospitals developed after about 1860 to serve rural populations that did not have easy access to the bigger towns. Small in scale, homely in character, they were supported by local general practitioners and charged modest fees. Eastbourne, Hastings, Crawley, East Grinstead, Horsham and Petworth all established them.It would seem that they have all since been redeveloped, although the free Homeopathic Cottage Hospital, established by Jane and Julia Leaf in 1888 on Marine Road, Eastbourne*, later transferred to a typical large Victorian house in the spreading suburbs. Although there have been later additions, the building on the corner of St Anne's Road and Mill Gap Road, retains a comfortable form suggestive of a cottage hospital, and the building today houses a dedicated clinical podiatry unit.

As she did with the official training of nurses, Florence Nightingale (*1820-1910*) gave a kick-start to the development of convalescent homes.

She was categorical, writing in *Notes on Hospitals* (1863):

> *It is a rule without any exception, that no patient ought ever to stay a day*
> *longer in hospital than is absolutely essential for medical or surgical treatment.*
> *What, then, is to be done with those who are not yet fit for work-a-day life?*
> *Every hospital should have its convalescent branch, and every county its*
> *convalescent home.*

In fact, Sussex finished up with quite a few.

Nightingale's initial idea was for a 'string of cottages' that would resemble a home more than a hospital, with small, but segregated, wards housed in simple, inexpensive buildings. In the end a variety of types and sizes were to be built as adjuncts to metropolitan hospitals, allowing the city beds to be freed for more urgent cases and giving patients time to recover fully. Doctors argued for country and seaside locations, and the pioneer Metropolitan Convalescent Institution chose Bexhill for a large seafront home. Other convalescent homes were built in Brighton, Eastbourne, Hastings, Hove, Seaford, Bognor Regis, Burgess Hill, Rustington and Worthing – with their clientele being brought from as far as Hertfordshire.

Getting better by the seaside

Of the surviving buildings, the most significant is the All Saints' Convalescent Hospital for the Sick Poor – to give it its original descriptive title – close to Eastbourne's[*] seafront, facing King Edward's Parade and Darley Road. Opened in 1869 and run by the All Saints' Sisters, it continued in operation as a hospital until late in the 20th century. Apart from the historic interest, the substantial original buildings, designed by Henry Woodyer (1816-96), are of real architectural note and have all been listed for conservation. The buildings are to be converted for residential purposes by the end of 2008, but with all the exteriors due to be restored and obtrusive 20th-century additions stripped away, so that the original form can be appreciated. Although the green space towards the sea is to be sacrificed for further homes, sightlines should still allow views of the façade with its arcades and first-floor balustrades.

The hospital building is a long brown-brick structure with a cross-wing. Mostly two-storey, it has further accommodation under a steeply pitched roof with projecting half-hipped dormers and a higher double-pitched roof at the centre of the composition. There are some distinct Gothic touches to the details, including stone-dressed windows with tracery, and a medieval-type stair turret with a conical roof tucked into the angle of the main building. The site also contains a large chapel, designed by the same architect and completed in 1874. This, too, is of brick with stone dressings and a plain tiled roof complete with bell-cote, but the Gothic elements are more strongly accentuated by the tall traceried windows, complete with the original stained glass. The High Victorian interior is notable for its multicoloured brickwork and special coloured encaustic tiles, and it is hoped that it will become publicly accessible after the redevelopment is complete. The site is bounded by a pebbled wall – a natural choice of material for a coastal location – banded with brick courses, and this contrasting combination is also incorporated in the appealing tile-hung lodge house on Darley Road.

The Rustington* Convalescent Home dates from 1897, and probably even better exemplifies what we think of as an appropriate residence for seaside recuperation – not least because it is still in use today. Situated on the Sea Road between Littlehampton and Rustington, it is set back behind wide lawns and flowerbeds, with the original wrought-iron entrance gates facing the sea. Designed by a local man, Frederick Wheeler, this is a handsome building with a broad façade of brown brick and six pairs of sash windows dressed in red brick on each of the two stories. A fine central tower with stone quoins rising above the roofline is surmounted by a clock and cupola, and there are pretty dormers in the attic. At one end there is a small wing with a terrace and balcony, but modern windows; at the other is a projecting wing with closely spaced windows, a classical-looking pediment gable and an octagonal turret with a conical roof at the corner. Altogether a very pleasing building, the simple prospect of which must encourage recuperation.

The former French Convalescent Home at Brighton* is not surprisingly, in a very different architectural style, but still one to delight. The building on Marine Parade, by the turning for Arundel Road, stands back from the road behind a neat lawn and gravel driveway. Recently restored and converted to provide flats, the central symmetrical part of the building was opened in 1895 to provide for patients from the French Hospital in London's Shaftesbury Avenue. Later two wings were added, but broadly in the same style. Although built with Belgian bricks, all the walls were later covered in cement render, adding to the unity of the building's appearance. The façade on the seaward side is three storeys with attic windows, the wings rising a floor higher. The French style is apparent in the steeply pitched, pavilion roofs with metal cresting and finials, a colonnade with round arches on the ground floor, and a pair of turrets projecting from the fourth floor of the wings. Not exactly a chateau, but clearly out of the ordinary along this stretch of seafront.

Specialist hospitals

For much of the period, the medical establishment had favoured general hospitals that dealt with the full range of acceptable cases and had frowned on the idea of colleagues specialising in particular areas of medicine. However, many doctors were determined to concentrate their research and practice on specific conditions, and the most ambitious of these found backers to establish specialist hospitals, although these tended to develop in the larger towns like Brighton where there was sufficient demand for the specialism.

The one specialist Victorian hospital that currently survives is the Hospital for Sick Children – now the Royal Alexandra Hospital for Sick Children – on the corner of Dyke Road and Clifton Hill, Brighton[*], which is due to be vacated in 2007. Apart from its historic importance, this 1881 building is also of architectural interest. It was designed by a local architect called Thomas Lainson, but very much in the 'Queen Anne' Revival style being promoted at that time by London architects such as Richard Norman Shaw (*1831-1912*).

The building was fitted onto a triangular site, with the widest frontage facing over the garden and the main entrance to the street given limited prominence. The overall design is both complex and intriguing, but still visually appealing. Lainson astutely avoided anything too institutional in appearance – after all this was a children's hospital – by giving a strong domestic flavour to the design. Of three storeys, built in friendly red brick, it has a nice variety of windows with moulded white glazing bars, and two projecting oriel windows on the street side. The garden side features a pair of gables with prominent chimneystacks rising through them, and a turret with an appealing lantern and cupola. Overlooking the garden, at the first and second floor levels, are glazed balconies added at later dates. There is also extensive use of terracotta as mouldings around the main door and the windows and for decoration, giving extra richness to the texture of the building. However, like the patients inside it, this is a currently a building in need of TLC – and more than a little restorative medicine.

The asylum age

The Victorian period also saw significant changes in the treatment of the mentally ill, though from a pretty miserable baseline. The hangover of attitudes to mental disorder from the 18th century and the absence of proper provision meant that the mentally ill would most likely find themselves incarcerated in prison or placed in the parish workhouse. Families that could afford it might make use of private 'madhouses', though here the conditions could be abysmal. Some counties, although not Sussex, established county asylums paid for out of local rates, but otherwise there was really only one charitable hospital for the mentally ill in the whole country – the Bethlem Hospital in London.

Following reformist agitation, and the report of an 1844 Lunacy Commission, legislation required all counties to provide asylums paid for out of the local Poor Law rate, and open to regular inspections. Private asylums were also to be registered and regulated. At that time it was reckoned that there were around 300 'lunatics' chargeable to the Sussex workhouse Unions. The Boards of Guardians paid for some to be kept in private asylums or the asylums of neighbouring county authorities, while others remained in the workhouses. But a good proportion were noted as being paid for to be 'with their friends or elsewhere'. This was presumably a form of care in the community. In any event, given that local ratepayers would bear a proportion of the cost, not everyone was in favour of new asylums. The Guardians of the Lewes Union even petitioned parliament about the unnecessary nature of creating a County Lunatic Asylum.

However, in 1859, a special asylum was completed on a large site at Haywards Heath[*]. Called St Francis Hospital, it continued in use as a psychiatric hospital until 1995 when it was renovated and converted for residential use. As a result this very remarkable building can now be seen in something like its original splendour; even if you don't respond to its striking style, its size and grandeur have to be recognised. Now known as Southdown Park, the buildings are approached via a driveway off Colwell Road, although the magnificent façade is on the other side of the building overlooking sports fields and countryside, with views to the Downs.

Designed by Henry Kendall Junior (*1805-85*) in what is known as the Lombardo-Venetian style, the building is distinguished by the extraordinary length of the symmetrical façade, the two substantial towers framing the central block, the ornamental campaniles at either end of the building and the striking use of polychromatic brickwork. The yellow brick has regular wide bands of red brick along the length of the building, as well as other decorative bands incorporating grey bricks. The windows are emphasised by being arched with red brick or an alternating pattern of red and yellow. The main entrance on the Colwell Road side incorporates the same characteristics, with additional decorative brickwork features and a set of carvings above the triple-arched entrance. Nearby is the very Italian-looking chapel with a tall campanile built in the same broad style, but with pointed Gothic windows and extensive decoration below all the cornices.

Out of consideration for the patients' needs, the asylum was located away from the town centre, with the rural position considered as beneficial for their treatment. Originally there were 400 patients in a self-supporting community that incorporated a number of the ancillary buildings that survive today. The whole ensemble remains today as a remarkable testament to mid-Victorian society's attempt to deal with one of their most vulnerable groups and the economic muscle they were prepared to apply.

Nationally, the number of mental patients grew 15-fold between 1847 to the end of the century, with the most problematic cases being sent to the county asylums, and many of the rest remaining as patients in the workhouse. During this period, attitudes to the mentally ill were ameliorated as a result of the work of medical reformists, and objectives became focused on cure rather than the simple containment – and sometimes restraint – of patients. Nevertheless it was estimated that only one in eight mental patients recovered as a result of medical support in asylums. Most patients were effectively left to themselves in communal dayrooms, the troublesome ones mistreated, and conditions for all were bleak.

Despite the increasing need, it was not until after the Local Government Act of 1888 and the creation of the separate counties that further asylums were built in Sussex. By then ideas about the design and layout had also changed; asylums were to be composed of a pattern of separate buildings with segregated wards for patients with different conditions and needs. They were also planned as self-contained communities, complete with workshops, a laundry, staff accommodation and an obligatory chapel.

West Sussex got its County Asylum as late as 1897, with a complex of buildings designed by Sir Arthur Blomfield (1829-99) at Greyingwell, Chichester[*]. It was built to house 800 patients in graded wards, designated as chronic, acute, quiet and epileptic, and remained in operation for a full century before closing. The future of the site and the buildings is currently under consideration for redevelopment. However, there are strong signs that a core of original buildings will be retained (for residential and other uses), with sufficient public access to allow visitors to get an idea of both the style and extent of the asylum. The parkland site is approached from College Road, with the driveway entrance called Connolly Way just opposite the end of Wellington Road; another driveway, Blomfield Drive, is further on in Summersdale Road. The most prominent structure is the massive water tower; having walls over two metres thick and being a Chichester landmark, it is unlikely to be removed. The main reception building next to it set the architectural tone for the institution. A red-brick building with a symmetrical façade in the classical style, it has sash windows with white frames and slightly protruding concrete quoins at the corners. There is a pediment gable over the central section, grey-slate tiles on the roof, red-brick chimneystacks and a central clock tower capped with a cupola. The other buildings nearby, some with dormer windows, are broadly in the same style. The exception is the Gothic-style, flint-faced chapel.

The East Sussex Asylum was established in 1901 at a typically isolated site outside the village of Hellingly. This, too, was a self-contained community built on a grand scale to house 1,000 patients. Apart from a large main block containing wards, the administration facilities and an acute patients' hospital, it featured detached villas for groups of patients, a block for disturbed children and an isolation hospital – as well as staff accommodation and a chapel. The hospital closed and many of the buildings were abandoned in the 1990s. The site, approached from The Drive just off Grove Hill, is currently due for redevelopment, and it seems unlikely that any of the interesting early buildings will survive.

Making room for the dead

Whatever the advances in medicine and improvements in hospitals, fatal diseases were still commonplace, the mortality rate in the country remained high and infant deaths were still a feature of the overall increase in population. Disposing of bodies became a problem. Parish churchyards had little space for expansion and urban churchyards became overfilled, causing genuine public health concerns. High-density internments involved coffins stacked in piles, with common graves for the poorest. Often town graveyards were adjacent to overcrowded dwellings, and rats exacerbated contagion. Working-class families kept decomposing cadavers at home while they raised money for coffins and funeral expenses; further infection was spread by the habit of widows kissing the bodies of their dead husbands.

In the major cities, some private cemeteries had been established by profit-making Joint Stock Companies that charged high fees for burial plots. But this didn't solve the overall problem and by the mid-century the crisis resulted in legislation allowing the creation of public cemeteries financed and operated by local town or parish Burial Boards. The cemeteries were to be large, well drained, and sited away from urban developments. The age of the Victorian cemetery had arrived in Sussex, and by the end of the century over two dozen had been built.

The growth of cemetery facilities reflected the increasing elaborateness of Victorian funerals. For the wealthier classes, the way of marking death became an expression of social status and financial success. Cortèges could involve glazed funeral coaches drawn by up to six horses each with a plume of black feathers, paid attendants swathed in black with tall silk hats, and carriages full of moneyed mourners in freshly fashioned black bonnets. All this required a parkland setting, wide tree-lined driveways, landscaped flowerbeds and a pair of funeral chapels — one being for the Nonconformists who had been excluded from churchyard burial. These, and any ancillary buildings, were almost invariably in the Gothic style.

Something of the dignity and ethos of these events is still apparent in a few of the Victorian burial grounds in Sussex, with the biggest cemeteries displaying the best memorials — elaborate family mausoleums, sentimental graveside statuary and skilfully carved headstones with fulsome epitaphs. The earliest, and most notable, is Brighton's[*] original private Extra-Mural Cemetery, which opened in 1851 on the Lewes Road. The local Burial Board established its own cemetery, Woodvale, on an adjacent site in 1857. Nowadays there is a combined road through both, and visitors can drive or walk the route in either direction. There are entrances to each section from the Lewes Road one-way system between Bear Road and Melbourne Street, and a further entrance up the Bear Road hill, close to the turning for Tenantry Down Road.[1]

1. *The cemeteries are open every day from 09.00 (11.00 on Sundays and Bank Holidays) and close at 17.30 during the summer (16.00 from October), and you can get a walker's guide from the lodge close to the Woodvale entrance.*

Hospital life – and death

For the early Victorians, admission to hospital would have been viewed with serious alarm. Wards were crowded, surgery conducted without anaesthesia and fatal infection prevalent. Foul air rather than germs were thought to be the cause of disease, so doctors argued for strong ventilation of wards. But without effective dressings, wounds healed slowly and infections spread. Blood poisoning killed as many as half of those operated on. Even after the introduction of ether and chloroform as anaesthetics in the 1840s, surgeons were still unaware of the need for absolute cleanliness. Once Joseph Lister had introduced antiseptics in 1865 and sterilisation of instruments became standard practice, the situation improved, and the voluntary hospitals also introduced beds to accommodate paying patients. With their greater success and growing knowledge, hospital doctors' reputation improved and medical students' education moved from the anatomy room to the wards and operating theatres. Finally, the development of X-rays for diagnosis at the end of the century gave patients a further boost of confidence in the hospital process.

Partly under the influence of Florence Nightingale, hospital design evolved with the introduction of pavilion wards, long, rectangular rooms cross-ventilated by opposing windows. Sanitary, washing and other facilities were kept separate, heating systems introduced and great emphasis placed on cleaning and hygiene – and mortality rates fell.

Conditions in the workhouse infirmaries were grimmest; trained nurses were not available, and doctors could be reluctant to accept posts in rural workhouses with masses of hopeless cases and mentally disturbed patients. Again it was Nightingale and the ladies of the Workhouse Visiting Society who played a part in reforming medical provision in the workhouses. Initially hospital nurses had low pay and low status, akin to that of servants, and were expected to sleep in, or overlooking, the wards, but Nightingale's influence and increased training ensured better, separate accommodation, even if organised on hierarchical principles. Trained matrons emerged with a key role in the hospitals, but only after overcoming the resistance of male doctors.

These are places to explore at leisure, full of fascinating memorials that vividly express Victorian attitudes to death. At the start of the Extra-Mural Cemetery Drive there is a flint-faced Gothic chapel with a tall stone-arched portico designed by the prolific local architect Amon Henry Wilds (*c.1790-1857*), who also laid out the cemetery grounds. Next to it is a notable mausoleum of knapped-flint with ornate, pointed stone arches, and niches containing sculpted biblical scenes and allegorical figures. There are numerous Victorian monuments embellished with sculpture and carving all around the paths of this lower section. You can almost hear the horses' even tread as an imagined cortège passes. At the top of the Woodvale Drive is a further pair of large, conjoined chapels, and between them a tall tower with a spire. These too are in the Gothic style, faced with Sussex flint and with elaborate stone tracery in the windows. However, the original central porte-cochère through which the carriages once passed has been blocked, and one chapel has been adapted to serve as a crematorium.

In general, it is the town cemeteries that are most rewarding to visit. Ocklynge Cemetery at Eastbourne*, on the A2270 Willingdon Road, is attractive and extensive, set on a sloping site with plenty of yews, conifers and other trees, with a good prospect across to wooded hill-sides opposite. The memorials date from the 1860s and include family tombs in the classical style, headstones with foliate decorations, statuary with praying angels and an elaborate Gothic memorial to an MP's wife. There is a pair of chapels, Gothic in style and faced with flint, and a keeper's house with rubble facing and pointed arch windows set in smoothly dressed stone.

The burial ground at Lewes* is also on a sloping site, and from the top there are pleasing views towards the downs. The original Victorian section of the ground is approached from Rotten Row, and just inside the gates is a pair of chapels in red brick with a high arched porte-cochère between. They have the usual Gothic elements of narrow, pointed lancet windows with stone surrounds, and small buttresses with angled stone caps. There is a Sussex touch to the rear elevations that are entirely hung with tiles. The earliest graves date from the late 1860s, and although not especially outstanding, include some fine ivy-clad family tombs, a couple of obelisk memorials, a weeping figure or two, as well as a few well-carved headstones.

The Victorian burial ground at Worthing[*] was established away from the town centre at Broadwater, with the entrance in South Farm Road. The cemetery, with memorials and sarcophagi dating from the 1870s, is largely unkempt, but invites exploration. With plenty of mature trees, lots of bushes and even blackberries to be picked, the grounds seem to be being reclaimed by nature. Ironically, the chapels at the entrance are protected as listed buildings, and the pair of them has been spruced up despite no longer being in use. These are in the usual form and Gothic style, but distinguished by the variegated colours of the rubble walls, and a smart turret and spire set on the roof.

Hove[*], too, had its own Burial Ground, established in 1882 on the south side of the Old Shoreham Road, with the railway line running along the other side. The entrance lies between the turnings for Amherst Crescent and Olive Road. This is an extensive, open space with a wide driveway and the usual pair of chapels, but generally lacking the character of the others, with the Victorian memorials somewhat scattered amongst later graves.

Internment remained the death ceremony of choice for most of the period. Cremation was frowned on or prohibited by religionists, and wasn't legally acceptable until after 1885. Even then, negligible numbers opted for the flames, and Victorian cemeteries continued to flourish well into the next century, remaining part of our, sometimes fading, national heritage.

CHANGE IN THE VILLAGES

NEW BUILDINGS FOR A NEW AGE

It will be apparent to anyone travelling around the Weald and Downland countryside of Sussex, that signs of the dynamic changes during the Victorian period are least in evidence in her villages. The obvious exceptions will be those touched by the railways, which will have swollen in form and function to take on a new status as small towns and commuter destinations. Here, rows of Victorian terraces, town houses and suburban-style developments – and everything that followed thereafter – will have swamped the original village form. But where villages have retained some reasonable approximation of their early 19th-century size and structure, it is easier to identify the standout buildings that indicate the impact specific Victorian initiatives had on these rural enclaves – schools, village halls, estate cottages and the occasional almshouse. Each form speaks of incremental shifts in the community, of piecemeal rather than convulsive change.

One set of changes, though, is less transparent, even if there are clear physical signs to be teased out from noting the topography of villages. The gradual process of field enclosure that had been going on through-out the country for centuries, was largely complete by the time of Victoria's accession, and had in any event been much less widespread in Sussex. However, legislation in 1836 and 1840 shifted attention from the enclosing of open fields, to permitting the enclosure of common lands, including the pasture, meadows and woods that the poorest farmers and villagers relied on to sustain a few animals or provide fire-wood. Even after the appointment of a Parliamentary Commissioner to supervise the enclosure of commons, and with powers to retain areas for communal and recreational use, the cottagers in the villages continued to lose many of their traditional grazing rights and small farmers lost land they had habitually cultivated, usually with only minimal compensation. The winners were the local large landowners who incorporated the commons into their existing holdings or sold them for building plots. There were some four-dozen such commons enclosures of various sizes in Sussex during the period, where only a village green or recreation ground remains as communal land, often fringed on one or more sides by houses erected in late Victorian or Edwardian times.

But one of the abiding contradictions of the Victorian rural elite is their capacity to claim for themselves with one hand, while giving away with the other. Most of the benefits noted below are directly attributable to the virtuousness of local aristocrats, landowners, squires and wealthy clergy who saw reason to contribute to the well being of their workers or the wider community of the village. The story of village schools (recounted on *pp.45-51*) is often the tale of generous initiatives by moneyed worthies providing land or initial finance for a school building – perhaps prompted by their belief in the value of promoting education per se, or their recognition of its capacity to instil or bolster established social relationships. Either way, they paid up front, and the underclass benefited.

Homes for the workers

Likewise, rich estate owners saw sense in providing better homes for their workers, labourers and tenant farmers, and there are some fine examples of their investment in estate cottages in various places in Sussex that are worth a look. Most village labourers lived in squalid conditions in poorly maintained cottages that might survive little more than two generations. With possibly only one or two rooms, these were cramped, crowded and fetid. The privileged hierarchy were alarmed by the conditions from both a sanitary and moral perspective. And as labourers began to drift away from uncertain rural occupations to find work in the coastal towns, to emigrate or 'tramp' their way to the industrial cities of the north, landowners might be prompted to provide decent tied housing to ensure a loyal, but subordinate, workforce. Nevertheless, since rents did not reflect the investment necessary for building anew, an element of philanthropy played a part in the equation.

Perhaps the largest and most complete set of Victorian estate cottages are those built by the Goodwood* Estate in the 1870s and 1880s. Known locally as Duchess Cottages, they were named after Frances Harriet, the sixth Duchess of Richmond, who may have encouraged their construction. Some four-dozen pairs were built, and they are scattered across a dozen villages of the ducal lands, with many of the cottages some distance from Goodwood House itself. Although there is no noble crest or insignia to identify them, they all have a similar and character-istic form, possibly stock designs chosen from an architect's ready-prepared selection. Most are of H-plan, two stories with the gables facing to the front, and with red-tiled roofs, a trio of chimneys and white barge-boards under the eaves. They are built with flint, distinctively set in serried courses – rather than casually laid – with a notched, short-and-long pattern of brickwork on the angles of the buildings and around the windows. A darker dripstone moulding above the windows adds a further distinctive element to some. These are substantial structures, still fit as modern homes, that must originally have provided comfortable quarters for the lucky labourers and their sizeable families.

The most concentrated collection of these cottages is around Lavant, across the fields from Goodwood House. There are two pairs in Mid Lavant* at the side of the A286, diagonally across from the Post Office stores; another pair across the allotments that face the little church on the bend in the main road; a pair on your right as you reach the edge of the village heading north, and two more pairs standing proud in the fields a little further on, just where the B2141 forks left towards Chilgrove. East Lavant* also has fine examples, a pair in Pook Lane, but another more prominent one facing the cricket green. Over at Oving* there is a further selection in the High Street. There are two pairs of the same general design, but with additional dormer windows, a distinguishing lattice pattern in the glazing, and slate tiling – probably from a later date. Notably they stand opposite a small estate of mid-20th century cottages that remind us of the continued need for homes for rural workers. Further along the High Street are a few more of Goodwood's Duchess variants, including a pair to which dormers have been added later, and an oddly narrow three-storey house with the lattice pattern glazing. Apart from these, if you want to play Hunt-The-Duchess, you can try spotting other examples in villages across the territory.

On a smaller scale, the village of Compton* is distinguished by a set of neat and homely-looking estate cottages, mostly set around a small triangle of green. These are mainly of flint with two storeys, and like the Duchess cottages they also have notched brickwork around the windows and brick quoins forming the corners. In addition they have a brick band across the façade and tiled canopies or porches for the front doors. The cottages are each dated and identified with initials indicating that they were part of the local manor of Geoffrey Phipps Hornby. Inscriptions on the cottages tellingly reveal Victorian attitudes to housing the labouring poor. One reads, 'The Sleep of the Labourer is Sweet', another has a more general aphorism: 'Peace Be Within These Walls'. A further estate cottage in a similar style at nearby Up Marden is dated 1861, and inscribed 'Rest and Be Thankful'.

Another major Sussex landowner, the Earl of Abergavenny, also provided workers' housing around his estate at Eridge Park*. These are smart and distinctive-looking pairs of two-storey cottages built using mostly red brick, but with contrasting yellow bricks patterned around the windows and corners of the buildings. They have a single, substantial chimneystack, ridge tiles with terracotta finials on the roof and similar tiling over the dormers and porches. They also have a distinctive decorative band of moulded terracotta rosettes around the building, but more particularly they carry the Earl's crest in high relief on the facades.

The cottages can be easily spotted beside the A267 at Frant*, and also a kilometre or so further south on the same road as you drive towards Mark Cross.

At Merston*, a low-lying hamlet just off the A259 between Chichester and Bognor, there are two pairs of estate cottages opposite the farm in Marsh Lane. Dated 1867, and well constructed with knapped flint and brick under red-tiled roofs, stylistically they resemble others in the area. This is hardly surprising given that by the 1830s there were numerous pattern books with ready-made cottage designs, and that after the introduction of the blueprint copying method in 1842, builders had detailed drawings available, with no need to interpret the pattern books. The availability of rail transport meant that bricks and timber could readily be transported from some distance, and the repeal of the brick tax in 1850 cut construction costs further. However, it is clear that some landowners still valued local materials and styles even after cheaper building methods became available.

Some estate buildings seem quite grand and hardly deserving of the title 'cottages'. At Flimwell*, on the A268 Hawkhurst Road and not far from the main junction with the A21, is a set of substantial and architecturally elaborate estate buildings (Seacox Cottages). Their style incorporates ground-floor stonework, Gothic windows set in brick, Tudor-style half-timbering and decorative tile hanging for the upper floors, and sinuously shaped bargeboards over the front porch, gables and dormers. There is even a brickwork pattern in the chimneystack at the side. This melange of styles might seem idiosyncratic, but simply reflected Victorian designers' propensity to draw on the past for architectural ideas. In any event, the size of the homes provided in the building suggests that they might have been intended for the landowner's agent or state manager rather than a lowly labourer.

The tiny village of Madehurst* appears to be centred on splendid Victorian estate buildings that create a delightful picture-book image. At the core of the hamlet is the flint-faced medieval church that was largely rebuilt in 1864. To one side is a pair of cottages, to the other the combined old schoolrooms and teacher's house; both of these traditional Sussex buildings are finely crafted, using the same materials and similar design. The flint facings are laid in courses with gallets — flakes of waste flint — pressed into the mortar, and the contrasting brickwork is used around windows, on the angles of the buildings and in the gables, as well as in bands and patterns on the façades. The gable eaves and dormer roofs are enhanced by finely scalloped bargeboards, and the roof of the schoolhouse has pleasing patterned tiling.

If most estate cottages suggest pattern-book architecture that could be readily replicated by a local builder across the landowner's territory, then one exception is a set of Cowdray Estate cottages in Midhurst[*] that form the corner of Edinburgh Square and St Ann's Hill. Given that they are near the original Cowdray House, it is perhaps not surprising that the buildings commissioned from the architect E.C. Lee in about 1880 are a bit exceptional as accommodation for estate workers. These are substantial-looking buildings of two storeys and attic rooms, with a solid stone base below the window line of the ground floor. Above this they are mainly brick with lots of neat, patterned tile hanging on the upper floor and gables. Well-formed archways on two sides, strongly figured brick chimneystacks, and doors and window frames painted in the Estate's distinguishing gold colour, add further visual distinction.

As at Midhurst, not all estate homes were in rural positions or of simple cottage form. In Arundel[*], the Duke of Norfolk built two terraces of homes in Bond Street. On the north side is a row of two-storey redbrick cottages with attics, individual porches and a bit of front garden. There are plenty of good details including elaborate tracery on the end bargeboards, Pulborough stone dressings and iron rainwater heads embossed with the red Norfolk lion and the date 1868. Opposite is an earlier, more modest two-storey terrace built in beach flint, with brick used for dressings and chimneys.

In Petworth[*], likewise, the Estate opted for terraced rows of cottages. The Egremont Row in Angel Street consists of six neat two-storey cottages built in stone with brick dressings, each having its own porch and garden to the front.

Village halls

Victorian landowners' benefaction also sometimes stretched to providing for the whole local community by building village halls, reading rooms or libraries. At Eridge* Green, the Abergavenny family endowed the village with an unpretentious Parish Room in 1884. Built in red brick, with a trio of windows and main door in the Gothic style – accentuated by surrounds in yellowish brickwork – it looks at first glance like a chapel. The building is tucked away in a cul-de-sac just off the A26 (take the turning from the main road towards Rotherfield, then immediately left), and is still in use by the local community today.

There is an altogether grander Village Hall at Forest Row*, in a prominent position in the centre of the village, just by the mini-roundabout. The symmetrical front of the T-shaped building looks more like a domestic residence – casement windows with leaded lights, traditional tile-hanging on the upper floor and tall red-brick chimney stacks at either end of the red-tiled pitched roof. However, a contrasting and projecting segment above the central porch combines half-timbering with white plaster and contains elaborate plasterwork with a gilded crest and dated dedication that tell the story of the building's origin – erected by Henry Ray Freshfield of nearby Kidbrooke Park in 1892. Behind, is the hall itself, red brick with small stone buttresses and a wide, pitched roof surmounted by a delicate lantern. John McKean Brydon (*1840-1910*), who had worked as assistant to two leading architects of the time, Richard Norman Shaw (*1831-1912*) and William Nesfield (*1835-88*), designed the building and the design certainly reflects their styles. The relative architectural flamboyance of a hall for a small village also suggests an architect trying to make a mark.

There is a similar quality of architectural elaboration in the combined Village Hall and Library building on another mini-roundabout in The Street at Cowfold*. Designed by the firm of Wheeler & Godman in 1896, this too combines various materials and visual elements that again suggest both domestic and civic functions. There is tile-hanging, Tudorish half-timbering, prominent bay windows, decorative swags in plasterwork and an octagonal lantern with a copper cupola – as well as two-tone brickwork and some mullioned windows for the hall itself. Perhaps it is an example of architects having fun with the stylebook, but still certainly a noticeable building.

Sir Aston Webb (*1849-1930*), a more serious designer, and a luminary of the Victorian architectural world, was responsible for the splendid Ticehurst* Institute, built in the 1899 at the eastern end of the village's High Street and originally financed from charitable funds. This was a village hall and more, having a public parish library, several function rooms and residential accommodation included in the ensemble under a composite series of pitched roofs. Largely red brick with tile-hanging above, the large hall and other main windows are divided by stone mullions and transoms in the medieval fashion. The main entrance is also of local stone, giving weight to the sense of an Institute, in what is a sophisticated building for a small village. Still very much in use today, the hall is equipped with a stage for local drama events.

The Queen's Hall and Library on the west side of the High Street in Cuckfield* is something of a village treasure. It's a sturdy-looking two-storey building constructed with smoothed sandstone blocks under a Horsham stone slab roof. Tudor-style mullions and transoms divide the windows on the ground and first floors, with a pair of blank windows in the gable above. The best feature is the well-formed and richly carved door case, above which is a lamp and an inscription with, slightly oddly, the date 1897-1901 – covering the Queen's Diamond Jubilee until her death.

Almshouses

Victorian benefactors in Sussex also continued an earlier charitable tradition of providing almshouses for impoverished village widows, worn-out labourers and the infirm elderly. There is a particularly fine example of the form at the Wood's Almshouses in Church Lane, Oving*. This is a neat and attractive row, very solidly built with flint facings, but also distinguished by the finely finished masonry surrounds of the windows and doors. Two projecting wings with gable ends pierced by pretty upper windows, more masonry dressings and three substantial chimneys reinforce the sense that this is a place of repose. Dating from 1839, the building has an adjacent companion in the same style in the form of a school, also designed by John Elliott. Although now in residential use, the exterior of the building, like the almshouses, appears little altered.

Seaford* boasts the more substantial-looking Fitzgerald Almshouses in Croft Lane, close to the High Street. These are mainly two stories, with knapped flint facings, red-brick dressings and stone lintels, but the distinctive feature is a three-storey castellated tower complete with an attached octagonal turret and cruciform arrow slits. This defensive form for an old folks' home seems incongruous – were they trying to repulse undeserving widows? – but probably simply reflects the Victorian fashion for medieval styles. Endowed by a local worthy and JP, John Purcell Fitzgerald, the almshouses were built not long after the railway reached Seaford, when the town was still much more compact and village-like.

Worthing* too has almshouses from its pre-expansion days. A detached pair on the corner of Humphrys Road and Portland Road is all that remains of the Humphrys Almshouses, though this is a fine enough building. Faced in dark, knapped flint, it has stone dressings and mullions for the windows, a steep tiled roof with cresting, chimneys over the gables and a large porch with open timberwork.

But the prize for 'Best Victorian Almshouse' in Sussex must surely go to the picturesque pair in Falmer*. Originally known as Knight's Almhouses, now called Pelham Cottages, they are situated at 1 and 2 Mill Street, on the north side of the village. Dated 1869, and display-ing the Pelham family shield, this is a seemingly perfectly realised single-storey building with two window-bays and a central porch, designed in the local Sussex style. So, lots of chunky flint, brickwork in notched shapes around the windows and corners of the building, partic-ularly finely carved and fretted bargeboards with hip-knobs, red roof tiles and well-figured brick chimneys. The judges awarded extra points for details such as the fine masonry windowsills and lintels with courses of brick in line with them, windows with latticed panes, and a hand-some brick-framed doorway with a pointed stone arch and drip-mould.

Had rural philanthropy been more prevalent, or the county's wealth more evenly spread, we might have inherited more gems like these. As it was, those that could provided what they would, and many villages retain to this day these practical memorials of the Victorian spirit of social munificence.

GAZETTEER

WHAT'S WHERE IN VICTORIAN SUSSEX

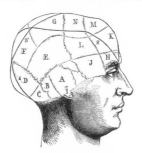